Pet Subjects

Animal tales from the *Telegraph*'s resident vet

Pete Wedderburn

The Telegraph

Aurum
Press

Brimming with creative inspiration, how-to projects and useful information to enrich your everyday life, Quarto Knows is a favourite destination for those pursing their interests and passions. Visit our site and dig deeper with our books into your area of interest: Quarto Creates, Quarto Cooks, Quarto Homes, Quarto Lives, Quarto Drives, Quarto Explores, Quarto Gifts, or Quarto Kids.

First published in 2017 by Aurum Press, an imprint of The Quarto Group. The Old Brewery, 6 Blundell Street, London N7 9BH, United Kingdom. www.QuartoKnows.com

A catalogue record for this book is available from the British Library.

ISBN 978 1 78131 615 3
Ebook ISBN 978 1 78131 709 9

10 9 8 7 6 5 4 3 2 1
2021 2020 2019 2018 2017

Typeset in Caslon and Gill Sans by SX Composing DTP, Rayleigh, Essex
Printed and bound in Great Britain by CPI Group (UK) Ltd, Croydon, CR0 4YY

Contents

Introduction

This book is about mysteries from my veterinary practice. I've been a vet for over thirty years, and I've been called to solve many puzzles. The following chapters document some of those memorable cases. Not all have happy endings, but they all have one thing in common: in every case, the mystery was solved. Nothing was left unexplained. For each story here, that answer may have been elusive, but it was finally found.

The life of a veterinary surgeon can be surprisingly similar to being a biological sleuth. A vet of our times is like a twenty-first-century Sherlock Holmes, investigating crimes against animal bodies. The difference is that vets are searching for the non-conscious perpetrators that cause disease, not criminals. These could be physical injuries, viruses, bacteria, or any number of assorted random causes.

Many people think that the main job of vets is to treat animals. In fact, this is the easy bit. The biggest challenge, and the most significant part of our work, is to make the correct diagnosis of the cause of our patient's illness. Once the diagnosis has been made, treatment is easy.

Sometimes the diagnosis is obvious: a skin laceration from running into a sharp piece of wire, a cut pad from standing on a sharp object, breathing difficulties from smoke inhalation in a dog that's been in a house fire, or overheating in a dog that was left inside a car on a sunny day. But often there's a mystery that needs to be solved. Is a cough caused by allergic lung disease, heart failure or an inhaled object? Is a dog's itchy skin caused by fleas, skin mites or an allergic reaction to pollens? Does a cat have sore eyes because of a viral or a bacterial infection, or is there an irritant in the environment causing a reaction? For every simple case, vets have to deal with half a dozen sick pets where the diagnosis is elusive. This is both the challenge and the joy of veterinary science. The frustration of not being able to make a diagnosis is countered by the satisfaction of finally discovering the unifying cause of a complex set of signs in a sick pet.

It's critically important that vets identify and deal with the root cause of animal diseases: the correct diagnosis of the cause of illness is fundamental to what we do. It's only by working out exactly what is making an animal unwell that we are able to move on to the next stage of our job: offering an owner a prognosis (the expected course of the disease) and giving the animal the best treatment.

If a dog has a swelling, there could be a hundred possible causes, each of which requires a different approach. An abscess requires drainage and antibiotics. A malignant cancer may need radical surgery followed by radiation treatment or chemotherapy. A swelling caused by an invading splinter may simply need to have the splinter located and removed. Without the specific diagnosis of the underlying cause, a prognosis cannot be given, treatment is just guesswork, and there's a high chance that the wrong approach may be taken.

Veterinary schools are adept at teaching vet students how to become detectives, how to search for clues, and how to gather as much evidence as possible. The underlying cause of any disease should be able to be identified using observation backed up by scientific tools of investigation. A newly qualified vet knows the theory of how diseases can be diagnosed: the veterinary equivalent of tracking down a criminal, and gaining a conviction in the court.

When vets go out into the real world of clinical practice, their veterinary education is topped up with daily experience. Every case is an educational experience, teaching the vet another possible manifestation of animal illnesses.

Vets repeat the same formula daily. We search for clues, gather evidence and solve the mystery by making a diagnosis. And then we use our experience combined with the experience of many others, as found in textbooks, for example, to give the most appropriate treatment for that particular diagnosis. The details of the veterinary investigative process are similar across the globe. Vets do this in a logical sequence.

First, before even looking at the patient, a detailed history is obtained. This means having a careful conversation with the owner, asking about the precise nature of the issue that they are having with their pet. When did the problem start? What, exactly, is their concern? What, precisely, have they observed?

Next, vets ask about the minutiae of the animal's life. What do they eat? How much do they drink? What are their personal habits? Do they enjoy exercise? Do they have any unusual foibles or idiosyncrasies?

Only once the maximum amount of information has been extracted from the owner can we move to the next stage: physically examining the patient.

The clinical examination has an almost spiritual significance in the veterinary world. Every vet has their own specific routine when doing this: the process must be done systematically, checking every aspect of the animal's physique. All of the five senses may be used: sight, touch, hearing, smell and even taste.

This last sense – taste – is rarely used, but I recall one example. When visiting a dairy farm, I had a habit of idly picking up a pinch of the cows' fodder, chewing the silage as you might chew a blade of grass. It had a pleasant, fragrant taste. On this memorable occasion, I had to spit it out: it tasted uncharacteristically bitter. On a hunch, I asked the farmer if the cows' milk yield had dipped recently. He nodded, looking at me strangely: how could I have guessed? After I'd explained, we tested the nutritional value of the silage. It turned out that it had undergone the wrong type of fermentation, spoiling so that it had 'gone off', and the cows were refusing to eat it. In small-animal practice, I have yet to use the sense of taste to make a diagnosis, although I occasionally taste medication to judge whether or not an animal is likely to swallow it willingly, and I have inadvertently had unpleasant taste experiences when foul secretions (such as anal sac contents) have accidentally squirted into my mouth.

Vets need to have an entirely open mind when carrying out a clinical examination, methodically recording everything that they notice. Small changes – a droopy eyelid here, a tense muscle there – can offer critically important clues, even if the significance is not apparent at the time.

Sometimes, on completion of taking the history and carrying out a clinical examination, a diagnosis can be made: the lame dog with a broken nail, the fighting cat with an abscess over his shoulder, or the rabbit with overgrown teeth. But in many cases, this is just the start of the diagnostic process.

Further evidence is frequently needed to discover the cause of the pet's problem, and that means that the vet needs to delve into his diagnostic armoury.

There are many ways of gathering more evidence, but there are two key weapons.

First, laboratory tests, using blood, urine, faeces, other bodily fluids, skin scrapings and biopsies. Such samples can be analysed using microscopes, cultures and a range of tests including chemical and now genetic analysis. The services of a clinical pathologist may be used: this is a vet who specialises in interpreting the evidence generated in the laboratory, piecing together the data to present a coherent answer to the puzzle.

The second big gun in our armoury is the broad area of diagnostic imaging, which has expanded dramatically in recent years. Technology is used to obtain detailed images of the inner goings-on of our patients. Radiology (i.e. x-ray pictures) is now supplemented by ultrasound, CAT scans, MRI scans and other new dynamic techniques.

Once vets have gathered all the evidence – from the history, examination and further tests – it should be possible to make that diagnosis. Sometimes it's straightforward: common illnesses are common. On other occasions, the mystery can be deep and complex, and for these vets need to use every available clue, apply every piece of knowledge that we have stored in our memories over the years. It can be a monumental challenge, but once the elusive diagnosis has been made, everything falls into place. The reason for the droopy eyelid and the tense muscle becomes apparent. The correct answer has been found, and the satisfaction for the vet is immense. The stricken patient can now be treated correctly, and the worried owner can be reassured.

For the veterinary clinician, there's deep intellectual and psychological satisfaction when the correct diagnosis is finally reached. It can feel like a sportsman scoring a goal, the successful lift-off of a rocket or finding a much treasured object that has been lost: it's an emotional high. Vets tend to be restrained, professional individuals, at least in public, but behind the scenes, I've witnessed colleagues high fiving and punching the air with delight when a long-standing clinical mystery is finally solved.

I'm grateful to my patients – and their owners – who have kindly allowed their stories to be told in this book. Following the requests of some owners, and for the sake of confidentiality, certain names and details have been changed, but the essence of the stories remains the same.

Thanks, too, are due to *The Daily Telegraph*, which has hosted my Pet Subjects column for the past decade, and to the thousands of *Telegraph* readers, who have asked me the fascinating animal questions that have challenged me. Some of my favourite queries are included in this book: I couldn't have answered them if they hadn't been asked, so thank you, readers, for asking.

1

The case of killer worms

One Sunday afternoon, I was driving home with my family after visiting friends. As we passed a patch of waste ground, one of my passengers called out: 'Look – there's a dog lying over there.' We stopped, and I went over to take a closer look.

The emaciated dog, a cross-bred mutt – perhaps Labrador and greyhound – was lying motionless on the gravel. She was young – no more than eight months – and clearly neglected. I went up to her, talking quietly, but she didn't react at all, just staring blankly into the distance. It was obvious to me that she was dying, but what was going on? Where had she come from, and what was the cause of her collapse?

I carried out a brief clinical examination. The dog's gums were a pale grey colour rather than the normal pink, and when I put my finger inside her upper lip, I could feel a deathly cold clamminess rather than the warmth of a healthy body. She needed urgent treatment, and even then, the chance of saving her life was slim.

We lifted her onto the laps of the three passengers in the back seat of the car. She didn't react in any way: she was passive and floppy, more like a sack of potatoes than a living animal. My clinic was closed, and the on-duty service was our local emergency clinic, a twenty-minute drive away. This was an ownerless dog who needed significant veterinary input, and I didn't feel that I could call on my emergency veterinarian colleagues to carry out this pro bono work when they were already likely to be busy with other cases. I decided to care for the dog on my own, at home.

During the short car journey home, the dog was named 'Finzi'. As often happens, her name seemed to pop out of the ether: it just seemed right. We later learned that Gerald Finzi had been a famous British choral composer, but there was nothing musical about this dog. She was simply a dying stray.

We carried her into our kitchen and settled her into a warm bed made up of a nest of blankets and hot water bottles, in front of our Aga. She lay there semi-comatose and floppy. At this stage, I asked myself if it would be kindest to accept that she was so close to death that it would be a mercy to nudge her over the edge. I petted her head, and talked to her, and at that moment, her tail flicked two quick wags. That was enough: Finzi had a personality crushed by neglect and disease, but she was still present and wanting to live. I left her in the care of my wife and daughters, and I called in to my vet clinic to get the equipment and medicines that she needed.

The most important, life-saving treatment was a blood transfusion: I could tell from her pale gums that she was anaemic. There was no sign of any external bleeding such as a wound, so the anaemia was most likely due to some sort of internal blood loss. I retrieved a bag of blood from the fridge at the clinic, and within an hour, this had been warmed up and was running into Finzi's circulation via an intravenous infusion.

Treating animals at home is never as professional or smooth as in a clinical environment. There are no veterinary nurses to assist, no consulting tables with non-slip surfaces, no packs of catheters and sterile swabs on hand, and no easy-access, easy-clean stainless steel kennel for the patient. Finzi was comfortable in her bed of blankets and hot water bottles, but it was awkward setting her up on a drip. I was down on my knees, hunched over her while my wife held her, raising her vein for me. Once Finzi had been set up with her life-saving infusion, I was able to pause to reflect on what might be the cause of her collapse.

The back story – or history – of a pet is always the foundation to searching for a diagnosis. She was a neglected young dog with an uncertain background. She was unlikely to have been given the standard preventive treatments that would be given to much-loved puppies. She had probably not been vaccinated against serious viruses like parvovirus and distemper, and these were at the top of my list of possible causes. I'd have to send samples to the laboratory to prove these infections, but her prognosis was appallingly bad if they were the cause, and she'd probably die before I had time to get results. She was also unlikely to have been given treatment for worms, and since these are almost universally present in puppies, it was very likely that she had a high worm burden. Finally, there are a number of bacterial causes of collapse, which could affect a poorly fed, rundown dog. I decided on a comprehensive treat-all home approach for the first twelve hours. If she was still alive at the end of that time, I could take her to my clinic and start a more systematic work up.

The blood transfusion was the centre of her care: as well as rehydrating her, and giving her much-needed red blood cells, this would also infuse her system with antibodies and other immune-system boosting biochemicals. I also gave her a comprehensive worm dose, and some intravenous antibiotics to help her battle against bacterial septicaemia.

Finzi barely moved for several hours, but there was a gradual, almost imperceptible improvement in her demeanour. She had closed her eyes and slept after we'd placed her in her warm bed, and when she woke up, she started to look around with some interest. When we talked to her, she looked into our eyes with a gentle brown-eyed gaze. And when we petted her, her tail began to beat a steady thump-thump of acknowledgement.

This stage is one of the daily sources of angst in a veterinary clinic: the delay while you wait to see if an animal is responding to treatment. For every dog like Finzi that begins to respond, there's another that doesn't. After doing everything possible, you never hear that reassuring thud of a wagging tail, you don't see a brightening of the eyes and there isn't any sign of improvement. Instead, life slowly ebbs out of the body. Passivity deteriorates into unconsciousness and finally into death. At the start of a course of treatment for a seriously ill dog, you don't know which way it's going to go. It can be an emotional rollercoaster: will you be in tears at the end of the day, or will you be feeling that surge of relief when you know your patient is going to survive? These are the highs and lows of working in a vet clinic.

At this stage, it looked like Finzi might be one of life's survivors, but we still weren't sure. I didn't need to take her to my clinic to carry out complicated diagnostics to find out the cause of her problem. After three hours of intravenous blood infusion, Finzi stood up, and with help tottered towards the back door: she wanted to go outside. As soon as the fresh air hit her, she vomited, bringing up a mixture of stomach fluid and clusters of wriggling spaghetti-like worms. Moments later, she passed a large volume of blood-stained diarrhoea, and this too contained fistfuls of long, stringy worms.

Finzi was the most worm-ridden animal I had ever encountered. She'd obviously never had the worming medication that's so important for puppies, and by eight months of age, her digestive system was loaded with the parasites. She had been able to manage until the worms had severely irritated the lining of her bowel, she had started to bleed internally, and she'd collapsed. If we hadn't found her, she would have died within a few hours.

Even then, I felt gloomy about her prospects. Once she had staggered back into her bed, she barely moved. The truth was sad and simple: her previous owner had neglected her, never giving her a worm dose, and now she was dying because of her overwhelming worm infestation. I gave her a comprehensive dose of wormer medication but I was worried that the worms had already done too much damage to her intestines.

Roundworms are astonishingly common in dogs. Mother dogs pass on worms to their pups in the milk. The worms in the pups settle into the intestines, growing into adults that damage the lining of the bowel. The larval version of the worm travels throughout the pup's body, and in female pups, some of them settle into the mammary glands, then when the female pup grows into an adult and has pups herself, those dormant worms are activated, passing on the worm infection to the new puppies in the milk. For this reason, almost all puppies are infected with roundworms, so to prevent the worms from causing serious ill health, repeated doses of a comprehensive worming medication need to be given at regular intervals.

Finzi didn't just have worms overwhelming her digestive tract. It was likely that there were also worm larvae wriggling through many tissues and organs around her body. My worm dose had come too late. She lay there, quiet and still. We stayed with her, talking to her, keeping her warm, and encouraging her to fight on.

For the first twenty-four hours, it was touch and go. Finzi just wanted to stay in her bed, and she had no interest in food or water. We kept her on intravenous fluids, changing from blood to electrolyte and glucose infusions, but her progress was slow.

She was still alive on the Monday morning, and I decided to keep her at home. Nothing extra could be done at the vet clinic: we knew what her diagnosis was, and I had given her the correct treatment. Her gums had regained a normal pink colour, so the challenge of anaemia had been conquered. It was now just a case of careful, caring nursing. We could do this as effectively at home as in a busy clinical setting.

On Monday afternoon, there was a small breakthrough. Finzi lifted her head and hesitantly ate a small amount of cooked chicken. She stood up again, walked unsteadily outside, and delivered another parcel of roundworms in a bloody pool of diarrhoea. Her intestines had been massively damaged by the worm burden, and I was still worried about her chances of recovering.

We sat up with her for a second night: my family had set up a rota of bedside care, taking it in turn to sit with her. If she became distressed, we wanted to be there to reassure her, and if the worst happened – if she died – we didn't want her to be alone.

With many seriously ill pets, there's a tipping point, and it can go in either direction. An illness can tip over the wall of an animal's defence systems, overwhelming the body. Or the immune system can rally against the challenge of the illness, restoring the bodily functions and returning the animal's physiology to a healthy state. Which way was Finzi going to tip, and when was it going to happen?

The corner was turned overnight: by the morning, Finzi had started to wag her tail spontaneously. We offered her some more chicken and rice for breakfast, and she wolfed it down. There was no more vomiting or diarrhoea and no more worms appeared. Later that day, she started to leave her bed on her own, wandering around the room wagging her tail. From then on, she improved rapidly and steadily, eating normal food within a few days, playing with our dogs in the garden, interacting enthusiastically with humans and behaving in nearly every way like a normal, healthy dog.

Finzi's recovery meant a happy ending for her, but unfortunately there was a sad twist to her story: three days after we'd rescued her, somebody found the body of a young male dog in the bushes not far from where she'd been found. It was Finzi's brother, also starved, neglected and abandoned. It was so sad to wonder if we had found him, could we have saved him too?

Finzi had soon fully recovered from her crisis, and we decided to keep her. We had two dogs already, but it was easy enough to fit in one more, especially a good-natured, gentle creature like Finzi. She found her forever home when we happened upon her that day. She has become a significant member of our family and we feel so lucky to have her. Four years later, Finzi is as healthy as any other young adult dog.

All adult dogs should be given a routine dose of worm tablets at least every three months. One thing is for sure: Finzi will never miss getting that dose for the rest of her life.

Questions and answers on digestive health

Finzi suffered from a common digestive problem in dogs. As the digestive system is a central part of the health and happiness of any animal, here are some further queries I've dealt with on the topic of digestive health.

We are now on our third golden retriever bitch. Our last one lived to be seventeen years old, and they have all been wonderful family dogs. Our one problem is that they are terrible at picking up and eating anything that they can smell (such as bird droppings) and this always seems to cause digestive problems. Apart from fitting a muzzle, can you suggest anything or do we just have to live with this?

KH by email

Dogs, having evolved as carrion eaters, have a strong instinct to eat now and ask questions later. You need to train your dog only to eat treats when you have given a command to do so. A remote-control training collar, which squirts an aerosol spray when you press a button standing thirty yards away, can be very effective (see www.companyofanimals. co.uk.). You start by teaching your dog to ignore treats that have been deliberately left on the floor. You do this by giving a squirt if she approaches the item without being told to do so. You then teach her to obey a command such as 'take it', to be used when there is food that you want her to eat. She should gradually learn that things are only 'safe' to eat if you have given a positive command to 'take it'.

> My dog was diagnosed three months ago with
> extended oesophagus, or 'megaoesophagus'.
> The symptoms were excessive salivating, coughing up
> food and water, and a lack of energy and weight loss.
> Having very nearly lost her to a bout of pneumonia,
> she is now staging a remarkable recovery. The advice
> I got from my vet, apart from raising the food and
> water bowls, was 'Try anything you think might help'.
> The information from the web was even more
> depressing, '. . . even with expert care, life expectancy
> is only two years'. I have tried a few different diets, and
> have found that Rice Krispies® seem to suit her best.
> She no longer coughs or brings back her food. She is
> only three years old. Do you have any other advice?
>
> GL by email

Every case of megaoesophagus has its own idiosyncrasies. Feeding from a height is essential, but there are different ways of making this easier, including specially designed doggy high chairs. As far as type of diet is concerned, some dogs do well on a liquidised diet, others canned food, others soaked dried food, and some on larger 'meatballs' of dog food. Every owner needs to go through a process of trial and error to find out what suits their dog. Rice Krispies® are not a good idea for the long term, since they will not provide a balanced diet for a dog. You should sign up with an online self-help group for owners of dogs with this problem – there are several helpful websites. I have one patient who has had megaoesophagus since puppyhood, and he is now a healthy seven-year-old, so don't give up! See also chapter 5.

I have had my seven-year-old Westie for three months and he keeps getting upset stomachs. I believe this is due to his preference for dirty puddle water over tap water. Is there anything available that may make tap water palatable to him?

CM, Bristol

Water from different sources may look the same to us, but to dogs, with their ultra-sensitive sense of smell, there may be dramatic differences in taste. Tap water is processed, sterilised with chlorine and contains numerous other organic and inorganic chemicals. It's safe for us (and dogs) to drink, but it's possible that a mild hint of chlorine to us could taste like swimming pool water to dogs. Many people use water filters to make tap water more pleasant for themselves, so you could try this. Alternatively, you could offer him cooled boiled water from the kettle. Perhaps the best answer would be to set up a rainwater collection barrel outside your house. The water that you collect will be the same as the water in the puddles but without the muddy contamination that could be upsetting his digestive system.

> My rabbit has been ill with a suspected hairball problem. The rabbit has recovered, and an experienced rabbit breeder suggested that papaya enzyme might help prevent recurrence. I also groom them and give them plenty of hay. Would it be safe to give one tablet to an adult dwarf rabbit that weighs just 1kg?
>
> *EC by email*

Hairballs are often blamed for digestive upsets in rabbits, but it's often more complicated than this. Rabbit stomach contents always contain some hair (and other fibrous material): this is normal. However, if the rabbit becomes dehydrated for any reason, the hair/fibre mix can become more solid. Rather than trying to break down the 'hair ball', it can be more beneficial to make sure that the rabbit is well hydrated, with plenty of fluids and a high-quality diet. To reduce the chance of such digestive upsets, I'd focus on providing a good balanced diet with regular dental checks from your vet to make sure that everything is being chewed properly. I don't think that it would harm a rabbit to have papaya enzyme given as per the label, but I'm sceptical about the benefits.

> My six-month-old rescue kitten produces foul-smelling gas. My vet doesn't seem to be concerned, but it's unpleasant at home. I feed him a mix of dry food plus some wet food from a sachet. His bowel movements are normal. What could it be and what can I do about it?
>
> *EB*

Excessive or unpleasant digestive gas production is often linked to the diet: some pet food ingredients produce a higher level of gas as they are digested. No company so far (that I know of) has been bold enough to market a 'low gas' diet, but you can obtain the same effect by choosing a bland, highly digestible food. Ask your vet to recommend one, or try a high quality premium range like Applaws (www.applaws.co.uk) or Thrive (www.thrivepetfoods.com). As well as being more easily digested, premium products tend to have the same ingredients from batch to batch, rather than varying depending on what's easily and cheaply available (which is what happens with many standard pet foods). If the problem continues after you have adjusted the diet, talk to your vet about probiotics to re-seed the bowel with healthier, less gas-producing bacteria.

2

The food-loving dog
who stopped eating

Jingo was a five-year-old chocolate Labrador who had two loves in life: people and food. It was always a pleasure to see him at my clinic. He would rush enthusiastically from the waiting area into my consulting room, wagging his tail at speed, and rush up to me to snuffle my hand. He made a welcome change from the many patients who can be understandably reluctant to come into a vet's room. I always felt that his friendliness was not entirely based on my likeability: I regularly use tasty treats to reward well-behaved pets. Jingo always made it clear that this was the highlight of his visit, continuing to snuffle my side with his muzzle long after he'd exhausted my supply of treats.

Jingo has not always had an enjoyable time at the vet. A few months ago, I didn't need his owner Chris to tell me something was amiss. Jingo arrived moving slowly, no bounce in his step and with his head down. His tail wagged feebly when I spoke to him and petted him, and he looked at me sadly before turning away from my offered treat.

'How long has he been like this, Chris?' I asked.

'It started after his afternoon walk yesterday,' Chris replied. 'He went straight to bed when we came home. When I offered him supper, he only had a fraction of his normal enthusiasm as I prepared his food, and when I put it down in front of him, he took a sniff then turned away. Jingo has never refused food in his entire life. I'm really worried about him.'

While he was talking, Jingo was slumped on the ground at Chris's feet. His body language said it all: he was feeling whacked. His habitual joyful exhilaration had evaporated.

'Has there been anything new or strange in Jingo's life in recent days?' I asked

'No,' Chris replied.

'Has there been any coughing, vomiting, or increased thirst?' I queried.

'No.'

'The only two abnormalities that I've noticed are his lack of energy and lack of appetite. He was great right up till that walk yesterday. Could he have strained his heart or something? He is always so energetic on walks, charging everywhere, chasing sticks and stones, pouring his energy into tearing around the place.'

I explained that dogs don't suffer from 'strained hearts', and that there was a long list of possible causes of his problem. The best approach would be to work through his case logically, and it was very likely that we would soon find out what was ailing him. And hopefully we could then get him back to normal.

I saw from previous notes that Jingo was fully vaccinated and had been wormed recently, which meant that viral infections or parasites were unlikely to be the cause.

As usual, the next stage was a careful clinical examination. As I lifted Jingo onto the table, he let out a quiet yelp. I frowned. How had I managed to hurt him? I had lifted him in the normal way, with one arm in front of his chest, and one arm behind his rump.

I started the examination. He had a mildly raised temperature and his heart rate was elevated, but otherwise his general parameters were normal. His limbs moved freely and comfortably, he had no pain in his spine, and none of his lymph nodes was enlarged. So far, so good. Jingo seemed to be, fundamentally, a healthy dog.

I moved towards his front end: I sensed from his yelp when I lifted him that the problem could be in this area. I gently prodded him around his chest, and while he didn't yelp again, he looked at me uncomfortably, as if he wasn't happy with what I was doing.

Next, I started to examine his mouth, and that's when the focus of the problem began to be clearer. Jingo refused to let me open his mouth. This dog would normally open his mouth as wide as possible, knowing that he'd probably be given a treat for doing so. Today, he kept his jaws clamped shut, giving me a sideways look through narrowed eyes as I tried to prise them open.

I tried a different tack, leaving Jingo's jaws shut while lifting up his upper lip and peering into his mouth from the side, between his teeth. That's when I saw a tell-tale streak of blood-stained saliva.

I turned to Chris. 'You said that he was chasing sticks and stones yesterday. Can you tell me more about that?'

'Oh that's what Jingo always does,' he replied. He finds anything handy in the undergrowth, hauls it out, and puts it down in front of me to throw for him. He then chases it and brings it back to be thrown again. He isn't fussy. He brings back stones as big as your fist or as tiny as marbles, and he likes sticks as small as your finger or as big as your arm. He just loves the chase, and anything will do.'

'And what did he chase yesterday,' I persisted.

'Well, he started off with a tennis-ball-sized stone, and when he got bored with that, he brought back a stick the size of a twelve-inch ruler. That was it. He lost interest in the games after that.'

I explained to Chris what I thought had happened: it seemed likely that Jingo had run on to that stick, spearing himself at the back of his throat. This is a common problem, and owners are often completely unaware of the risk.

The sequence of events is simple. Dogs learn to chase the stick with a type of wild abandon, racing after it at top speed, and seizing it as rapidly as possible. They then carry it back to their owner to have it thrown again, and again. Some dogs almost fall into a trance as they do this, chasing, retrieving, chasing, retrieving, over and over. There's no time to stop and think: it's all go, all the time.

The stick nearly always lands flat on its side on the ground, allowing the dog to grab it side-on in their jaws. The problem happens on the rare occasion when the stick spears into the ground at an angle, like a javelin. The dog does not have time to notice the difference, and so the stick is grabbed in haste as usual. However, because one end of the stick is fixed in the ground, the free end of the stick does not budge, while the dog's momentum carries the animal's body forwards at pace. It's as if the dog has run onto a sword held by a gladiator. The free end of the stick pierces the dog, lacerating the back of the throat. In rare cases, this can cause instant death, if one of the major blood vessels at the back of the throat is punctured. More commonly, the dog is badly injured, with the added complication that the injury is not visible from the outside, so owners are often not aware of the problem.

I had a strong suspicion that this is what had happened to Jingo. The only way to find out was to physically inspect the back of his throat. He was still refusing to let me open his mouth, so I would need to give him a sedative to relax him enough to let me see what was happening. My plan was that if I confirmed that this was what had happened, I would then deepen the sedation to general anaesthesia to allow me to repair the laceration.

Chris gave me permission to proceed, and he patted Jingo on the head as he left him with me. 'We'll soon have you hungry again, mate,' he told him.

After sedating Jingo, I was able to open his mouth enough to part his front jaws by around 10cm. This was enough to allow me to see to the back of his tongue with my torch. I could see strings of blood-streaked saliva: there was no doubt that Jingo had suffered some sort of physical injury to the back of his mouth.

Next, a nurse helped me to give Jingo an injection to induce general anaesthesia. As this deepened him into a state of controlled unconsciousness, I was able to open his mouth widely. I inserted a plastic endotracheal tube into his windpipe and connected him up to a gas anaesthetic system, which would keep him asleep while I attempted to repair his injury.

As I passed the tube, I could see the full extent of the stick injury. The laceration was 5cm long, just to the right of midline; if it had been just 1cm further towards the centre, Jingo would not have survived because of the major blood vessels that would have been severed. As it was, he had a nasty cut at the back of his throat, but his vital structures had been spared.

My job was to repair this cut, but before I did that, I had to check for debris such as wood fragments deep inside the wound. It's important that such foreign material is removed before a wound is stitched up, since it prevents full healing. As far as I could tell by gentle probing, there were no fragments in the wound, so I flushed it out with sterile saline, and began the painstaking work of suturing the wound edges together. This arduous work is a bit like trying to change the fuse of a plug at the back of a drawer that won't open: it has to be carried out under conditions of poor visibility and access. I had placed a spring gag in Jingo's mouth, so that his jaws were held apart, and a vet nurse was holding his head so that I had the best possible angle for access, but it was still not easy. I used an absorbable suture material so that there would be no need for sutures to be removed. I had to carefully place around fifteen sutures, and I was happy with my work. The laceration was now barely visible. The raw, painful edges of the wound were now pressed up against each other, and healing would already have started.

Jingo was given a powerful cocktail of pain relief, and he was allowed to wake up slowly over the following hours. By late afternoon, he was up and about. I was pleased to see that his tail was already wagging, and he had started to snuffle the hands of my vet nurses, looking for attention and comfort.

I had set him up on intravenous fluids: he would not be able to eat for at least a day, and I wanted to ensure that he didn't get dehydrated. He stayed in our clinic for thirty-six hours: by the next evening, he was sufficiently strong and energetic that I felt there was nothing to be gained by keeping him any longer.

Before Jingo left to go home, I carried out one final, important test. A nurse offered him a tablespoonful of moist top-quality dog food. Jingo didn't just sniff it and lick it, he dived on the spoon, and I'm convinced that if she hadn't been holding tightly to the other end, he might have eaten it as well. Jingo was definitely on the mend.

He went on to make a full recovery, but from then on, his life changed in one significant way: he was never again thrown sticks to chase. Chris now always goes out for walks equipped with a special sturdy ball and a hand-held ball launcher. Jingo has never been a fussy dog, and he loves running after the ball, again and again and again. The difference is that there is no risk of the ball landing badly and damaging Jingo's throat. Jingo has a new, safe game, and this one is never going to risk his life in the way that that simple piece of stick managed to do.

Questions and answers on throat problems

Jingo's damaged throat nearly became a life threatening issue. The throat is a key part of a dog's anatomy, as the entrance to the body for food and air. I'm often asked questions about throat problems, and here are a few examples.

My fourteen-year-old Labrador Jemma has started to make a strange sort of throaty noise. She makes a coughing sound and seems to be trying to bring something up but is never sick. My vet is at a loss to know what it is and has tried antibiotics but it still continues. It happens several times a day. Do you have any idea what this could be?

JA by email

There are a number of possibilities, but unfortunately it's impossible to make a diagnosis without asking your vet to do further investigations (or ask for a referral to a specialist for these to be done). Tests could include x-ray pictures of her neck and throat and having her respiratory tract checked thoroughly with an endoscope (a flexible tube with a glass-fibre core that we can peer through). A common cause of these signs in an older Labrador would be laryngeal paralysis, when the muscles of the larynx stop working, causing narrowing of the upper airway. An operation may sound like an extreme option for an older dog, but if this diagnosis was made, surgery could completely cure the problem permanently.

> My thirteen-year-old Labrador/German shepherd has started coughing. She has a spasm of three or four coughs before making a loud retching noise. After this she returns to her usual bright self. I mentioned this to my vet, and after a check-up of her lungs and heart, I was told not to worry, as old dogs do cough. Is there any treatment that I should be giving her?
>
> *FP by email*

While it's true that many older dogs suffer from a range of low-grade chronic diseases that can cause them to cough, such as bronchitis or laryngeal disease, it isn't 'normal' for any dog to cough. The problem is that the investigations needed to make a specific diagnosis can be complicated – and expensive. Blood tests, x-rays and ultrasound, and ultimately the collection of a fluid biopsy sample from her lung tissue, may be necessary. For this reason, some people prefer to accept that their dog has an occasional cough. If the cough gets worse, there may be no alternative and you may need to request a full work up so that an accurate diagnosis can be made, and the most appropriate treatment can then be given. Meanwhile, there are various general anti-cough medications she can take that may ease her discomfort; you should talk to your vet about which would be most appropriate.

> I have an eleven-year-old female Egyptian Mau cat named Aby Lyn who has lost her miaow for the past six months. She opens her mouth but is silent. I have taken her to my vet twice: they could see nothing amiss and decided, as she is well in herself, not to subject her to further tests that might distress her. Should I be worried?
>
> *JL, Leamington Spa*

The source of the cat's miaow is the same as the source of human voices: the larynx. The most common cause of a lost miaow is inflammation of the larynx caused by laryngitis, due to a viral infection, but this usually resolves within a few weeks so it seems less likely in this case. There are many other possible causes, including problems with the nerve supply to the larynx, and physical abnormalities around the larynx such as tumour-like growths. The only way to diagnose these conditions is to visually inspect the larynx under general anaesthesia, so perhaps it is time to discuss this option with your vets.

We have had a rescue cat, George, for three months now, and he has settled well. However, he seems to have no voice at all. We have not heard a single 'miaow' from him. When he is hungry, he goes silently to his bowl. If he wants to go out, he sits by the door and waits patiently. We find this a little unnerving, especially as our other cats have all been very chatty! Is there anything wrong with George?

MB, Somerset

The cat population varies in vocalisation in the same way as the human population. A few cats are always 'talking', miaowing loudly at any opportunity, and using their voices very effectively to get human attention whenever there is a human within earshot. Most cats are more focused than this with their voices, only miaowing when they need something such as food or access outside. George seems to belong to that small group that chooses not to vocalise at all. It is likely that he has the ability to miaow, but he has learned that his silent presence is enough to get what he wants. I suspect that one day, when he really wants something and you have not noticed his desire, you might just find that this strong, silent cat can talk when he needs to.

3

The interrupted cat nap

Jackson was a petite, perfectly formed ginger cat. He had a small spherical head, tiny pointed ears and long, bristly white whiskers. He was three years old when he started to cough. His owner, Kath, told me that he had always been prone to spluttering after eating, but when he began to cough in between meals they grew worried. He slept in a cosy basket at the 'living end' of their large kitchen, and normally he'd snooze all day, undisturbed. When he started to cough, he'd wake up, sit up and look around. He was now doing this four or five times a day, and it was upsetting him. After all, a cat needs his beauty sleep.

When I examined Jackson, he was breathing at around forty breaths per minute, twice as fast as an average cat, and I could see his sides heaving as he did so. When I listened to his chest with my stethoscope, I could hear an increased crackling, hissing sound in his lungs. It was obvious that there was some sort of lung pathology going on, but what was it? I took him in to my clinic for a work up to try to find a few more clues as to what was going on.

The standard investigative process for this type of case involves two procedures carried out under anaesthesia. First, I took a series of x-ray pictures of his chest. Four views were needed: two from the side-to-side perspective (one with him lying on his left, and one on his right) and two from the up-and-down perspective (one taken top to bottom, with him lying on his chest, and the other with him lying on his back, giving the bottom-to-top view). The different body positions cause the air in the lungs to move in different ways in each x-ray picture, giving subtly differing views of any changes inside the thorax.

The x-rays gave me the diagnosis I was looking for. Jackson's small airways were narrowed because their lining had become swollen and inflamed. This narrowing was preventing the free flow of breaths in and out of his lungs, causing air to accumulate in his lungs, giving them an enlarged, over-inflated appearance. And I could see tiny white circles (so-called 'doughnuts') caused by cross-sections of air tubes whose walls were thickened by inflammation and fluid. There were also 'tramlines': parallel white lines caused by a side view of these thickened air tube walls. These radiographic signs were typical of allergic airway disease, known as feline asthma.

The second procedure involved gathering some fluid from Jackson's airways. He already had a tube in his windpipe, as part of his anaesthesia, so I passed a smaller endoscope down this tube, used a viewing port to ensure I was deep inside one of his airways, then squirted in half a teaspoonful of sterile saline, before immediately sucking it out again. I transferred this sample into a small plastic vial, and sent it to the laboratory for analysis.

The result a few days later was as expected: Jackson's lungs were teeming with inflammatory cells of the type stimulated by an allergic reaction. This was further confirmation of the diagnosis of asthma.

I explained the background to Kath: 'The sequence of events in feline asthma has been carefully researched. First, a cat's allergic reaction to tiny particles in the air causes the cells lining the airway to produce excess mucus. The walls of these airways become swollen due to the inflammatory reaction, and the tiny muscles that control the airway diameter go into spasm, causing narrowing. All these changes result in an inability to inhale as deeply as normal, an inability to exercise properly and, of course, the coughing that you noticed. And just as the signs of asthma are caused by narrowing of the airways, treatment is aimed at widening them.'

'So how can we do that?' Kath asked.

'The cornerstone of treatment is to lessen the inflammation in his lungs by using anti-inflammatory drugs. These can be given in three ways: by tablets (if he'll take them from you), by injections or, ideally, by using an air mask.'

'You mean, like a human asthma puffer. Are you joking?'

I showed Kath an example of the AeroKat puffer: it uses a spray aerosol device like those used in humans, containing anti-inflammatory steroids, but instead of expecting a cat to suck on the device, it attaches to a large soft funnel which is gently held to the front of a cat's face. Not every cat lets their owner use this, but Jackson barely flinched as I tried it out on him. Cats have to sit still, breathing in and out seven to ten times after the aerosol button has been pressed, and Jackson didn't seem to mind doing this. The advantage of the mask-supplied inhaled drug is that the steroids go straight to the site of inflammation, bypassing the blood stream, so there are far fewer side effects. He'd need to have this done twice daily, and I supplemented the mask with daily steroid tablets at first. Once the asthma has been controlled, most cats can stop taking the tablets, with their condition controlled just by using the mask.

I also explained that Kath would need to review Jackson's home environment: there was to be a strict no-smoking rule in the house ('We have that already'), she was to use dustless cat litter ('He doesn't have a litter tray – he likes going outside'), and no fragrance or other sprays were to be used inside at all.

Jackson's treatment started well. Compliance was good (i.e. Kath managed to use the mask and give the tablets) and Jackson's cough seemed to happen less often. But two weeks later when I would normally be keen to reduce the daily tablets, Kath told me that he was still coughing several times a day. She wondered if other drugs could be added in, such as the bronchodilator tablets that an asthmatic friend of hers used, or maybe some other types of puffers.

I hesitated. Something did not feel right to me. I had made the diagnosis, we had started the optimal treatment, yet he wasn't responding nearly as well as I'd expected. I was reluctant to start down the road of more, stronger drugs at this stage. I began to wonder if I had missed something. Why was he not improving as much as he ought to be?

Kath lived in a big old redbrick house that I cycled past on the way to work every day. I had a simple suggestion. 'Instead of starting straight onto the new drugs, can I call by tomorrow morning so that I can get a full understanding of your daily routine. You know, the way you give the tablets, hold the puffer, and all that stuff. I just want to be sure that we aren't missing something in the way he's being treated.'

I arrived shortly after 8 a.m., and Kath showed me what she did. She gave Jackson a small meal of moist cat food from a sachet, then she sat down with him on her lap, holding him firmly as she gave him the dose from the puffer. Then before offering him another small portion of cat food, she held his mouth open while she deftly slipped the steroid tablet to the back of his tongue.

'Well? Do I pass?' she asked.

I was just saying that she had done everything as well as it could be done, when Jackson walked from his food bowl to his bed, which was a wicker basket lined with a baby's soft quilt, at the far end of the kitchen. There was an Aga stove beside his bed, turned off for the summer months, but obviously it would create a warm focus for the room in winter: an ideal place for a cat's bed. Kath had clearly taken to using the Aga as a centrepiece in the summer as well: there was a large peace lily plant on top of the stove.

'How long has that plant been there?' I asked her.

'Oh, ever since I turned off the Aga for summer: about two months. It was upstairs in the bathroom before. Why?'

Jackson had been coughing for just under two months, and this plant was right above his bed. I could almost visualise pollen from the plant drifting down into his breathing space all day.

'I think the peace lily might have to go back to its bathroom home for a while,' I told her.

The result of moving that peace lily was astonishing. Jackson improved dramatically within twenty-four hours, and the cough had vanished within a week. He was so much better that I suggested that Kath could reduce, then stop all the medication. The cough never returned.

Peace lilies seem like innocuous plants: even their name is calm and soothing. But pollens and dusts from any source can provoke allergies. After Jackson's case, I started a new approach to every chronically coughing cat. I now ask owners to take a short video of their pet's living area using their mobile phone. I haven't spotted another peace lily to date, but I'm not going to take any chances.

Questions and answers on respiratory diseases (coughing, sneezing and spluttering)

Respiratory disease, like Jackson's cough, is often seen in pets, and it can present in many different ways. Here are some of the questions that I've answered previously about coughing, sneezing and spluttering animals.

My dog, a Norwich terrier aged fourteen, has been coughing for about six months. The cough is harsh and deep and it seems to get caught in his throat. He has to stop what ever he is doing and just cough as hard as he can. When he gets excited he coughs, or when he is just walking down the road he coughs, and now he coughs in the middle of the night. There is no set pattern to his coughing. I took Buffy to the vet, and he has suggested antibiotics and steroids but I am reluctant to go down this path. I have tried homoeopathy and aromatherapy to no effect. Can you guide me in a new direction?

BEA, London

There are many possible causes of coughing, and to give effective treatment, a specific diagnosis does need to be made. X-rays of the chest and an ultrasound examination of the heart are often necessary, and other tests may also be helpful. In an older dog that is otherwise very well, chronic bronchitis is a possible diagnosis. If he does have this, there are some drugs like bronchodilators that may help, but they are unlikely to be enough on their own. I can understand your reluctance to use systemic steroids (i.e. tablets) but perhaps you might consider an aerosol inhaler that delivers steroids directly to the lungs, minimising any effects on the rest of the body (see www.breatheazy.co.uk to read testimonials from pet owners who have been helped by this treatment).

Can cats get hay fever? My six-year-old moggy has been sneezing a lot recently and I know it has been a bad pollen season. She is up to date with all her jabs and is otherwise fine and lively.

HB, Alderney, Channel Islands

Cats can suffer from allergies to pollens, and while the specific human signs of hay fever (sneezing with runny eyes) are unusual in cats, it's certainly possible. More common signs of allergies to particles in the air (like pollen) include coughing (feline asthma) and itchy skin, especially around the head and ears. Other common causes of sneezing include low-grade chronic respiratory virus infections (even in some vaccinated cats) and foreign bodies lodged in the nose (google 'grass stuck in cat's nose' to see what I mean).

If the sneezing is bothering her unduly, you need to get your vet to have a look at her: even if it's just an allergy, anti-inflammatory medication should ease the symptoms.

> Our seven-year-old golden retriever Oliver suffers strange episodes when he cannot catch his breath – he repeatedly snorts. Our vet tells us that it is 'reverse sneezing' and that we should just sit with him, reassuring him till it's over, but it can go on for several hours. Is there nothing else that we can do to help him?
>
> *PH by email*

Reverse sneezing happens when the structures at the back of the throat become tangled up with each other in the wrong orientation. It's harmless, but can be distressing. It usually sorts itself out within a few minutes, but if not, you can try gently pinching his nostrils together. This will stop him breathing in through his nose, so that he has to breathe in through his mouth instead. The idea is that this will re-orientate the structures at the back of his nose and mouth, so that they move into the correct position, and he will breathe normally again.

> One of my five-year-old guinea pigs snores at night. He breathes quietly in the day time but I can hear him from ten yards away when he's asleep. Why could this be?
>
> *WD, Cornwall*

44

Snoring is caused by an upper respiratory obstruction of some kind, so you need to work out why this might be happening. Guinea pigs are prone to allergies, which could cause upper airways to swell and narrow. He could be reacting to bedding in his hutch: it's worth trying a different type. Guinea pigs can also get respiratory infections, worse at night because of the enclosed air space in the sleeping area. If it continues, ask your vet.

4

The three-year itch

There's something about wire-haired terriers like Ned that commands respect. He had a solid, lean, muscled body, a boxy head and a stocky stance, as if always ready to resist being asked to move. Terriers are perhaps the most determined and stubborn of dogs, yet they combine this toughness with charm. When Ned developed serious skin disease, his natural characteristics of resilience and strength of character were needed more than ever.

Suffering comes in many forms, but severe itchiness must be one of the worst. Ned, and his owner Joseph, had nearly reached the end of the road. Joseph felt that the poor dog was in such discomfort that life was no longer worth living, and euthanasia was the only fair answer. As Joseph explained the background to the situation, Ned's head was dropped low, and he stared into the distance. He wore a large white plastic lampshade-type collar to stop him from chewing himself until he bled. His body was covered in reddish, balding areas, with thickened, sore-looking skin. Every half minute or so, Ned sat down and scratched his side with one of his back legs. If you touched his back, he would scratch frantically at the place you'd touched. It was obvious that his skin felt intensely itchy all over.

Ned had been brought to see me for a second opinion, and I had read the detailed case notes sent on by his first vet. Joseph was ready to let his small friend go, but his wife had convinced him to visit a different vet for a completely fresh approach. I had initially strongly suggested that instead of a regular vet like myself, they should consult a specialist dermatological vet, but Joseph's wife insisted he brought Ned to see me. Apparently I had cured her neighbour's cousin's dog of an itch five years previously, so she believed I had some sort of secret knowledge about fixing itchy skin.

Ned had been eight years old when the itchiness started, and at first it had seemed like a simple summer itch. The vet had given the usual short-term treatment, with anti-parasite treatment, some soothing baths and anti-inflammatory medication to relieve the itch. The drugs hadn't worked as well as expected, so a full dermatology work up had been done, to rule out other causes of itchiness. This had happened in three phases.

First, he'd been sedated, and a series of skin scrapes had been taken, to search for the microscopic parasites that can burrow into the skin, causing severe itchiness. None had been found. Second, under general anaesthesia, a skin biopsy had been taken, to allow a pathologist to scrutinise the changes in his skin at a cellular level, using special stains and a high level of magnification. The conclusion was that Ned was suffering from 'primary idiopathic superficial perivascular dermatitis and folliculitis'. Translated for the lay person, this exotic-sounding diagnosis meant that Ned was suffering from red, sore skin of an unknown cause. The skin biopsy had ruled out some important possible causes, but it hadn't helped discover the underlying reason. The most likely remaining diagnosis was some type of allergic skin disease, and the third phase of the diagnostic challenge was to find out what was causing his allergy.

Allergens can be found in three main areas: something the dog is eating, something the dog is coming into contact with directly, and something dust-like floating around in the air. For each of these, the ideal way of making the diagnosis is to remove the substance that may be causing the allergy, then to see if the dog improved.

Food-based allergies are usually the easiest to sort out. Ned was put on a special diet that was made up of hydrolysed protein, which has amino acid chains so short that they could not provoke an allergic reaction. Joseph was told to feed nothing at all but the special diet and water for six weeks. If Ned had a food allergy, he'd improve on this regime.

At the same time, a similar approach was taken to the possibility of an allergy to something that he was directly contacting. His soft blanket was replaced with simple brown-paper bedding. He was banned from carpeted rooms, and confined to lino-coated floors that were washed only in detergent-free warm water. He was exercised only on tarmac, kept away from grass and beaches.

After six weeks on this 'exclusion' regime, Ned was as itchy as ever. He had also been on antibiotics and shampoos to help with the secondary skin infection, and sprays to help to soothe the itchiest areas. Joseph was beginning to feel exasperated. The bounce in poor Ned's step had gone, and he rarely wanted to play any more. The plastic collar was now in daily use to stop him from making himself worse.

It was time to look into the third possible source of allergens: dust-like particles floating in the air. There are two ways of checking if dogs have this type of allergy: the gold standard has always been an intra-dermal skin test, where possible allergens are injected into the skin and the reaction is measured. More recently, a blood test has been developed which measures a type of antibody to the various allergens: this has been shown to correlate well with the traditional skin test, and it's easier to do. Ned's vet had carried out this analysis, and the results were disappointing. Ned was borderline-allergic to a wide number of common pollens and dusts. If he had been exceedingly allergic to only two or three particles, he could have been given immunotherapy, where tiny amounts of the offending allergen are injected under his skin over several months: the idea is that his immune system gradually learns to tolerate the substance, and the allergic reaction dampens down. When there are six or more allergens that are only marginally positive, it's unlikely that immunotherapy will work, and it's also questionable whether the allergens are even the main cause of the itch.

Despite this result, Ned's vet had decided to give a trial treatment with anti-inflammatory medication. Surely this would give the poor dog some relief. He started with the traditional approach, using a drug called prednisolone, but the side effects affected Ned badly, causing severe gastro-enteritis. The next stage was an anti-inflammatory drug that had only recently arrived on the market, with many cases being dramatically helped by its effects. Ned did seem marginally less itchy on this drug, but he still needed to wear his collar, and his skin still looked red and sore.

It was at this point that Ned had been brought to see me. As I looked at the unfortunate dog, and scanned the long and complex history of his previous vet's efforts, I had a panicky feeling of helplessness. His previous vet had done everything that could be done. I was trying to explain this diplomatically to Joseph, when to my surprise, the big man suddenly started sobbing. 'I'm sorry', he spluttered. 'I just can't cope with living with Ned any more. It's just too upsetting to watch him. I think I'm going to have to say goodbye to him.'

It was then that I had one of my strangely inspired thoughts. As I said the words, I hadn't even thought through what they meant in practice: 'If he can't live with you, why can't he live with me?'

Now that I thought about it, this was an entirely logical idea. We were fairly sure that Ned was allergic to something, and that meant that he was being exposed to that substance every day in his life with Joseph. So if he was removed from that environment entirely, there was a reasonable chance that any exposure to the unknown allergen would stop. One of my own three dogs had recently died, so my home had a dog-shaped niche: I could easily cope with another dog for the four to six weeks that would be needed. If Ned didn't stop itching, we'd at least prove that he wasn't allergic to something in Joseph's home.

We agreed that total separation was best: Ned would live with me, and there would be no contact with Joseph or his wife, apart from a once-weekly Skype video call.

Ned settled in well, tolerating the playfulness and jostling of my own dogs. He had his own allergen-free room, and was fed on the special hypoallergenic diet. He came on walks with me and my dogs, again sticking to tarmac only. He was a biddable, friendly dog, and I enjoyed having him around.

It can be difficult to judge the progress of long-standing cases, but at the end of week one, I could tell Joseph that Ned seemed a little better. Privately, I thought it might be wishful thinking on my part, but by the end of week two, Ned was definitely improving. By week four, I was able to leave him without his collar on, his skin no longer looked bright red, and his fur was beginning to grow back into the bald areas. We had definitely solved this case, but the real challenge lay ahead: what would happen when Ned went back to Joseph's house? Would the problem start up as severely as ever when he was exposed to the mystery allergen again?

We waited the full six weeks before allowing a reunion, and again, Joseph was in tears. This time, however, the emotion was joy. 'He's back to the old Ned,' Joseph gasped. His skin looked almost normal now, with not even an occasional itch from his back legs.

I had told Joseph that he had to scrutinise his home extra carefully, checking for possible allergens. No cut flowers, no perfume sprays, no dusty furnishings.

Joseph had done this, and as he left, he commented, 'I'm afraid that Ned's going to be very upset with me when he gets home. I've run out of his favourite dried-venison strip treats. He's had one twice-daily since he was a pup, but for the first time ever, my deer-hunting friend has run out. Ned isn't going to be happy.'

My mouth dropped open. 'Do you mean to say he has always eaten venison? Even when he was on his special diet?'

Joseph nodded. 'He likes them so much. How could I say no?'

The mystery had finally been solved. Venison allergy is exceptionally rare, but it was definitely the cause of Ned's itch. He never had another strip of dried venison in his life, and neither did he ever itch again.

Joseph felt bad about the part he'd played in Ned's saga, but I reassured him: he isn't the first owner to have held back information from a vet, nor to have failed to carry out instructions rigorously. He hadn't known enough to understand the significance of continuing to give Ned his so-called 'treats'. The message for other owners? Remember to tell your vet everything, and if you can't do everything the vet asks you to do, be honest about it. Don't try to hide anything: your pet is the one who may suffer if you do.

Questions and answers on skin diseases

Skin disease is one of the most common reasons for pets to be taken to the vet, from itchiness to baldness to strong smelling coats. There's always a reason for the skin going wrong, but it isn't always easy to find that reason. Here are some of the questions I've answered previously about skin problems.

I am a single woman in my mid-twenties, with a Siamese cat, Freddie. He has a problem with allergic skin disease, and he needs regular injections of steroids. The problem is that there are four vets at my local practice, and one of them is around my age, and very good looking. When he is on duty, I find myself stammering and blushing during the consultation, which is very embarrassing. I would find it less stressful to see the other vets, but I don't want to upset this vet by asking not to see him, because I think he is just adorable. Any ideas?

PK, Oxford

Perhaps this would be a better question for Ruby Wax or Graham Norton! Most vets are not offended if a client asks to see a different vet. They understand that there are many different reasons for personal preferences. You should ask to have a quiet word with one of the receptionists, and tell a small white lie, such as that Freddie gets stressed by the vet you wish to avoid. Many practices have systems that allow client records to be flagged with the preferred choice of vet, so if you make your choice clear on one occasion, you shouldn't need to keep repeating it. Do continue to smile charmingly at the good-looking vet from the safe distance of the waiting room if you see him. The ethics of a vet–client relationship are probably less complicated than the doctor–patient equivalent!

> We moved to the north east of Scotland two years ago with our three-year-old black Labrador Meg. Last summer she developed hair loss from her stomach up to her neck and also on the insides of her legs. Her hair grew back in during the winter. This summer the hair loss has been greater than last year. She enjoys two good walks a day in typical Scottish countryside, with long grass, heather etc.
>
> *C&LB, Grantown-on-Spey*

Hair loss, known as alopecia, has many possible causes. A referral to a veterinary dermatologist is the best way to solve this type of problem, but the distribution you describe (on her underside) together with the seasonal nature of the hair loss (in the summer) is very suggestive of a contact sensitivity or allergy. Her skin may be reacting to plants and flowers that are only present in the summer months. Next year, try avoiding the long grass and heather, and see if that helps. Or you could try a protective Lycra® body suit for her (see www.k9topcoat.com). She will look quite silly on her hill walks, but it can be very effective.

Our one-year-old golden retriever, Daisy, has had dandruff since she was a puppy. She's never been itchy. We have since tried dietary supplements of plenty of raw vegetables and an oil-of-evening-primrose capsule once a day, but the dry flaky skin is as bad as ever. It doesn't bother her but when after grooming her, we end up covered in dry flakes of skin, as does the floor. What else can we do?

JS by email

There is a dandruff-like skin disease that's common in Golden Retrievers called icthyosis. It's seen from puppy-hood onwards, and a skin biopsy is needed to confirm the diagnosis. Talk to your vet about this possibility. A referral to a dermatologist may be worth considering. Icthyosis and other causes of flaky skin are often not 'curable', but the worst of the flakiness can usually be controlled. You need to make sure that there are plenty of oil supplements in the diet. One capsule of evening primrose oil is not enough and you should consider adding in fish oils. Ideally, use a dietary oil supplement designed specifically for dog's skin (e.g. see www.lintbells.com). Regular shampoos will also help, using medicated products designed to help flaky skin. Your vet should be the best source of these.

> We have a six-month old Labradoodle puppy and he really smells doggy. Is there anything we can do to help him to smell sweeter?
>
> *SL by email*

It's normal for dogs to produce scented secretions that send other dogs messages about themselves. These are produced by glands under the tail, and also in the skin, especially around the ears, and the feet. In most dogs, the smell is not strong enough to be picked up by humans, but some dogs have a stronger than normal 'natural' smell. Skin and ear disease – and in particular a common yeast infection called malessezia – can also produce a noticeable fusty odour. Start by washing your pup in a dog shampoo and changing his bedding once a week. If this doesn't work, you should check with your vet. An ear infection may need treatment, and if malassezia is suspected, there's an excellent shampoo called Malaseb that should eradicate the odour.

My pet hamster, Hammy, has developed a balding,
itchy area on his back. It looks like the skin disease
caused by an allergy that my white West Highland
terrier used to get: it took many visits to the vet
and continual medication to get her sorted.
Could Hammy have the same type of condition?

KW by email

Any animal can suffer from allergic skin disease similar to
that seen in dogs, but it's pretty rare in hamsters. There's a
common skin mite that's often seen in hamsters: if this is the
cause, simple and effective treatment is available from your
vet. The vet may first wish to confirm the diagnosis by taking
a small skin scraping: the tiny mites can easily be seen under
the microscope. Other skin disease, such as ringworm, or
an irritant reaction to something in the environment (such
as hutch cleaner or straw bedding) are also possible, but are
less likely.

5

The giant dog who refused to budge

James was the Canadian owner of dog that was perfect for somebody of his nationality: a large Newfoundland called Trudeau. Trudeau was typical of his breed: the term 'gentle giant' may be a cliché, but it summed him up. He weighed over 60kg, yet he never exerted the strong influence that his size and power could allow. He was a well-behaved dog, always calm and quiet, even when confronted by annoying, yappy terriers or by the large, pushy boxer in the local dog park. He loved his daily walks, but he was a jogger rather than a sprinter, lumbering around at a steady pace.

Trudeau was four when his owner noticed that he was becoming more and more lazy. First, he stopped jogging, slowing down to a steady walk on his visits to the park. Then he decided to stop altogether. He seemed enthusiastic at the start of the walk, but just ten or twenty yards from the car, he would begin to sit down, firmly refusing to budge. There was little James could do. When 60kg of dog refuses to move, nothing can be done.

Even when James turned back, it was only after twenty minutes of pleading that Trudeau would agree to move at his own pace back to the car.

When this first happened, James thought that it might just be a one-off, so he gave Trudeau a break from his walk the next day, then he tried again. This time was worse. James called my clinic from the spot, and brought Trudeau straight to see me.

When I first heard James' account of what had happened, my first concern was that the big dog might be suffering from heart disease. Cardiomyopathy, when the heart muscle stops contracting properly, is a common problem in giant breeds of dogs, and sometimes the early signs of a problem include exercise intolerance and weakness. But when I listened to Trudeau's chest with my stethoscope, his heart sounded clear, strong and regular. While it was still possible that the problem could be an intermittent cardiac issue, it seemed unlikely. I racked my brains: what else could cause this large animal to suddenly develop acute, debilitating inertia?

The rest of my physical examination of Trudeau was not enlightening: he was a normal, slightly overweight Newfoundland dog. I could not find any hint of a physical abnormality. This was a puzzler. Could he just be 'being lazy'?

I decided that a detailed history might throw up some clues, so I asked James about every tiny aspect of Trudeau's life. Where did he sleep? What sort of food did he eat? What kind of food and water bowls did he have? What did he do during the rest of his day? Had anything changed in recent times?

The only unusual aspect of his life I discovered took me by surprise: James had a particular way of feeding him. He used a special frame for his food and water bowls, so that they were held at head height for Trudeau. Someone had told him that it was difficult for giant breeds of dogs to eat from ground level, as the food has so far to travel uphill from the mouth to the stomach. So from an early age, he had used a frame designed for the purpose. Trudeau was used to eating from this, and it seemed to work well.

I couldn't see how this could link with Trudeau's current problem, but I made a mental note of it. Anything that was different from a 'normal' situation could be worth remembering.

There were no other clues, but I still felt that it was too soon to find the big dog guilty of 'laziness'. I set up two initial strands of an investigation. First, I took blood and urine samples for routine screening, carrying out analysis of a wide range of biochemical and haematological parameters to get a clear picture of the workings of his metabolism. Perhaps predictably, everything was normal.

Second, I booked Trudeau in for a day of diagnostic imaging. We started off with an ultrasound screen, to double check his heart function, as well as getting an overview of his abdominal organs. Again, everything was normal: no hidden internal issues that could be causing him to slow down so dramatically. We then moved on to take a series of x-ray pictures of his chest and abdomen. Sometimes this type of extensive work up can seem over the top. In the veterinary world, it's called a 'fishing expedition'. We are not looking for anything in particular; instead, we are checking everything and anything, hoping to find something that might explain what's wrong. It's like throwing bait on a fishing line into a pond, hoping to catch a passing fish.

Once the last x-ray had been taken, Trudeau was taken back to his large walk-in kennel. He had been fasting when he had been brought in: this is usually done in case an in-patient needs to be sedated or anaesthetised. Now that the work up was finished, one of our nurses noticed him looking hungrily at another in-patient who was eating his dinner. She felt sorry for Trudeau, and after asking me for permission, she gave him a small bowl of bland dog food. Trudeau scoffed this hungrily while standing up, but it was then that something peculiar happened. He made a type of belching sound, and he brought up the food onto the kennel floor in front of him. He seemed puzzled by this, and before the nurse could stop him, he had eaten the regurgitated food from where it had landed. This time he lay down immediately after eating, and he seemed to settle.

I had only seen him do this out of the corner of my eye, because I was preoccupied with looking at his radiographs. And I had just caught my fish. There was something odd on his chest x-rays.

The finding was subtle enough but it was there all right. The interpretation of x-rays is an area of veterinary practice that has always fascinated me. The blacks, whites and greys of the image are like a hazy impression of the insides of the animal, but they are all entirely logical. Early in my career, I felt frustrated with my inability to read the subtleties of some x-rays, so I'd gained an extra qualification in the skill of x-ray interpretation. This had served me well over the years, and Trudeau was another example.

His chest x-rays clearly showed the white shape of his heart, surrounded by the blackness of his air-filled lungs. But there were two strange parallel black lines running across his lungs, from left to right, around 10cm apart, like the marks that a pair of skis might leave in the snow. I knew that there was only one possible cause of these: a distended, floppy gullet caused by a condition called megaoesophagus. This finding tied in exactly with what I had just witnessed: dogs with megaoesophagus often regurgitate their food, because their gullet doesn't have the muscle power to push the food from the mouth all the way into the stomach.

The interesting aspect of Trudeau's case was that by chance, his owner was already giving him the treatment for megaoesophagus: feeding from a height. This allows gravity to carry the food into the stomach, lessening the chance of regurgitation. James had accidentally been covering up his dog's problem.

So Trudeau definitely had megaoesophagus. But how could this be connected with his recent episodes of laziness?

When James came to collect Trudeau that evening, I told him that I wanted to go for a short walk with the two of them. There was a simple test that I wanted to do: the plan was to exercise him until he lay down, and then to give him an injection of a particular drug that might act as an antidote to the problem. We went into the car park, and Trudeau, perhaps keen to go home after a day in an unfamiliar place, set off at a pace towards the far end. He had nearly reached the gate when he flopped down. 'See,' James said, turning to me, 'that's exactly what he does. He'll refuse to move now for at least twenty minutes.'

I nodded, then reached into my pocket and took out a pre-loaded syringe. I slipped the needle into the vein in Trudeau's front leg, and gave him half a teaspoonful of the syringe contents.

I had warned James that he might jump up after I'd done this, but I could tell from his expression that he was sceptical. 'Will it really work quickly?' James asked, but before I had time to answer, he was dragged off. Trudeau had leapt up, and he had headed out of the gate, with James struggling to hold him back on the lead.

On their return, I spelled it out for James. Trudeau had a rare condition known as myaesthenia gravis, an immune-mediated disease of the neuromuscular junction (the microscopic site where the nerves pass on their impulses to the muscles). For unknown reasons, the immune system develops antibodies against the receptors at this junction. The result is that the muscles simply stop working after short episodes of exertion. The muscles of the oesophagus are also affected, which is why megaoesopagus is also seen in most cases.

The most rapid way to diagnose the condition is to give an injection of a drug called edrophonium, which has a rapid effect of restoring normal muscle contraction and strength at the neuromuscular junction for a short period. The test is not absolutely specific, but in the circumstances of Trudeau's situation, I was satisfied that the diagnosis was highly likely. A follow-up blood test to measure antibodies against the receptors was needed. A fortnight later, the results from the blood sample sent to a reference laboratory in California came back and it was no surprise when they confirmed the diagnosis. I had been so confident that I had already started Trudeau on the treatment, and to our relief, he had started to respond.

His treatment involved tablets three times daily, using medication that modifies the biochemistry of the neuromuscular junctions. Studies have shown that over 80 per cent of affected dogs can recover spontaneously if they are helped through the acute phase of the illness by these drugs.

Within just a couple of days of starting the tablets, Trudeau had started to enjoy his walks properly again. James ended up keeping him on the medication for a full year, and then he gradually phased out the tablets. Trudeau remained well, and the problem never recurred: he lived to the grand old age of twelve, which is impressive for a giant breed.

James continued to feed Trudeau from a height, and I was left wondering how much of a difference this made to the dog. The most serious complication of myaesthenia gravis is inhalation pneumonia, caused when regurgitated food is inhaled into the lungs. This is the most common cause of death in the cases of the condition that do not do well. It was possible that James had accidentally protected his dog from this fate in the early course of the disease because of his unusual idea of feeding his big dog from a height.

Questions and answers on muscle and nerve issues

Trudeau's diagnosis was a rare condition, but questions about muscle and nerve issues in pets are common. Here's a selection from my weekly column.

As many people know, domestic animals walk on the diagonal, one outside and one inside leg at a time, whereas camelids, i.e. camels, llamas and alpacas, use two outside legs followed by two inside legs.
My German shorthaired pointer seems to contradict this. When she is confined to a slow gait (e.g. on a lead) she paces like a camel. Once back to trotting speed she reverts to the diagonal. I have never seen a domestic animal do this and wonder if it is normal.

VT, West Sussex

It can be difficult to work out exactly what animals are doing with their legs because movement of four limbs happens so quickly, even when just walking. To do proper gait analysis, you need to take a video, and replay it in slow motion so that you can see exactly which feet are on the ground at any given moment. Pacing, by definition, has suspension and is done at a trotting speed. If your dog is doing this gait at walking speed, she could be using an 'amble', with three feet on the ground at a time, but it can be difficult to spot this without video analysis. Pacing is not a 'normal' gait of the dog and it can be a fault if they do it in the show ring, but many dogs do pace when restricted from trotting by being on a lead. It doesn't do any harm, and it isn't a sign of anything to worry about.

> I'm hand-rearing a kitten that I found alone beside the road: she was only a few days old. She's now two weeks old, but she can't stand up. Her legs go out to the side like a frog's legs. My vet says that she's a 'swimmer' and he tells me she has a good chance of getting better. Is he just being kind to me? Would I be better to accept now that she's not going to walk, and just have her put down?
>
> MC, Newcastle

This is rare in kittens, but 'swimmer pups' are common, and they do often respond very well to simple treatment. The problem seems to be that the muscles that hold the legs in the standing/walking position are slow to develop. Simple steps to assist in muscle development are often all that's needed, including putting on little ties to hold the legs in the right position, and carrying out home massage and physiotherapy. Many affected animals are completely normal by the age of two or three months. Success is not guaranteed, but it's definitely worth doing your best for her.

My two guinea pigs have developed a strange gait, so that they shuffle around and their legs aren't moving normally. What could be wrong? I haven't been to the vet because it's a farm-animal practice that isn't used to small fluffy pets.

HH, Devon

You need to take them to the vet as soon as possible. All vets are given good basic training in the wide range of animals that are kept as pets and will easily be able to give your pets the treatment they need. The most common cause of these signs in guinea pigs is vitamin C deficiency, which is why all guinea pigs should be given a diet rich in fresh vegetables. As a routine measure for all guinea pigs, a daily dose of 50mg vitamin C in a commercial form should be added to the food or water if there's any doubt about the adequacy of the diet. Your guinea pigs may now need a series of vitamin C injections from the vet to ensure that their joints recover.

My four-year-old miniature schnauzer had an embolism, which has left her with a paralysed left front leg. A programme on television recently showed how some paralysed dogs have been treated successfully by the injection of something taken from their noses. Is it possible that my dog could receive this treatment?

JW by email

The recent study at Cambridge University (www.vet.cam. ac.uk) involved transplanting a special type of cells (olfactory ensheathing cells) from the lining of the nose into the spinal cord at the site of damage that had caused the dogs in the study to become paralysed. Many of the dogs that received the transplant showed considerable improvement and were able to walk on a treadmill with the support of a harness, whereas none of the control group (who had a neutral fluid injected into the injury site) regained the use of their back legs. This is tremendously exciting, but it's not a treatment that's likely to become generally available (for animals or humans) for several years.

6

The cat with a gravelly cough

Nero was a black cat with the personality of an emperor. As his owner, Kath, explained his problem to me, Nero sat in a composed position on the consulting table, regarding us with an expression of disdain. He had a glossy black coat, a lean muscular body, intense green eyes. He was a big cat, resembling a small puma, in his prime at five years of age.

Kath explained that the problem had started the previous evening. Nero had been sunbathing in the garden all afternoon: it had been a fine summer's day, and he liked to stretch out in the flowerbeds, basking in the sun. Kath had been gardening when she came in from work, and she had heard Nero cough. He had never coughed before, so she was immediately concerned. She went over to him, and he was sitting up in the flowerbed wearing a puzzled expression. He then coughed again a few times, extending his head forwards, with his neck stretched out. He seemed to feel better after this, starting to groom himself while glancing at Kath, as if to say, 'What are you looking at?'

Kath presumed that he had inhaled some dust that had caused a temporary irritation, so she didn't think more of it at the time, but later that evening, the same pattern was repeated. Nero was curled up in his basket after supper, when he sat up, stretched his neck forwards and coughed. Again, he coughed two or three times, then he stopped, stood up, and went for a walk outside. Kate reckoned that he must have felt the need for fresh air.

Then the following morning, exactly the same pattern repeated. There were two episodes, with Nero coughing violently then returning to apparent normal breathing. Kath brought him in to see me for a morning appointment.

There are many possible causes of coughing in cats, from heart disease to respiratory viruses to direct irritation (e.g. by inhaling an irritant vapour) to asthma (as with Jackson, caused by allergies, see page 35). The history that Kath had given me suggested that this was a sudden onset problem, but because some long-term diseases can present in this way, I kept an open mind about what could be causing his problem.

When I examined Nero, there wasn't anything unusual to find: he was as strong, bright and haughty as usual. I opened his mouth, peering into his throat, and everything looked healthy. I listened to his chest with my stethoscope: his heart was clear and regular, with no irregularity, and his lungs sounded normal, with no crackles or extra noise.

I was about to suggest that perhaps this had been a minor temporary respiratory irritation that had resolved, when Nero pushed his head forwards, extended his neck, and coughed loudly. He did this two or three times, looking very uncomfortable. He recovered straight after, sitting upright and glaring at us.

The respiratory tract is difficult to examine thoroughly in the consulting room. The outside of the body can be visually inspected, as can the oral cavity. The head, spine and limbs can be manually palpated, and even the abdomen can be checked by using one hand to squeeze the abdominal contents, feeling for swellings, painful areas or other abnormalities. The chest, however, is protected by the rib cage, so the lungs can't be seen or felt. In a vet practice, x-rays are the quickest, easiest and most cost-effective way to get more detail about the state of the lungs. From the way he was coughing so violently, it seemed likely that something was causing a direct irritation to Nero's breathing passages. The most rapid way to move towards a diagnosis was to take an x-ray picture of his chest.

Unlike humans, cats will not voluntarily position themselves correctly when having an x-ray taken; to hold a cat in position would expose veterinary staff to an unwanted dose of radiation. For this reason, safe reversible drugs are used to sedate cats enough for them to be gently manipulated into the correct position, then held in place using tubular sandbags with rope ties.

Kath left Nero with me, and I gave him the sedative injection. One of my veterinary nurses stayed with him as he felt the impact of the drug. His imperious expression softened, he settled into a sphinx-type pose, then he lay his head down between his front legs. He had the appearance of sleeping, but it was an artificially induced state of sedation.

I rapidly took two views of his chest with our digital x-ray machine. This is standard practice: one view just gives a single perspective (e.g. side to side, or up and down). Two views are essential to allow visualisation of the entire contents of the chest, and to be able to establish the precise location of any abnormalities.

The x-ray pictures can be seen within less than two minutes, and I was shocked at what I saw. The cause of Nero's cough was now so clear that even somebody without veterinary training would be able to see it. There was a bright white oval shape, around the size of a small marble, right in the middle of his lungs. There was only one object that could look like this: a small pebble. While Nero had been stretched out in the flowerbed, he must have accidentally inhaled a small stone. His body had attempted to remove this via the coughing reflex, but it had not been successful. The stone was now deep inside his lungs, and it had to be removed. Nero would continue to cough until it was gone, and there was a risk that its presence could provoke an even more serious reaction.

Removal of the stone was a challenge. There were two options.

First, I could pass an endoscope – a flexible tube with a glass fibre core that we can peer through – down Nero's windpipe into his lungs, then use a grasping device to grab the stone, and pull it out. However, I knew that in practice it can be difficult to grab hold of small smooth spherical objects. They tend to slip and roll away from the endoscope, and it would be easy to accidentally push the stone even deeper into Nero's lung.

The second option of thoracic surgery was more radical: to open Nero's chest, cut into the lung and directly remove the stone. I would need to refer Nero to a specialist centre for this surgery. There was nothing easy about it, and it would involve risks for Nero.

I was just reflecting on these options, when my nurse called out to me: 'Nero's turning blue.' I ran over to her: he was still on the x-ray table in his sleepy, sedated state. His chest wall was moving in and out, but it was obvious that oxygen was not reaching his lungs, and he was dying of suffocation. There was only one possible cause: the stone must have moved slightly, perhaps because of the relaxed state of his sedated musculature, and it was now causing a complete obstruction of his main airway. There was no time to get the endoscope, and not even time for emergency surgery to cut directly into his lungs. Nero was going to die within minutes if I could not save him.

There are occasions when the text book stops being relevant, and impulsive direct logical action is needed. That pebble had to come out of Nero's lungs immediately, and I could only think of one way of doing that.

I grabbed Nero from the nurse and, holding him in my arms, rushed out of the x-ray room, along the corridor, and out of our clinic door. As soon as I was in the open air, I held Nero's back legs with both hands and began to spin him like a windmill, whirling him round and round. It only took three turns: I heard the crack as the stone from his lungs flew out, bouncing off the clinic wall. I then rushed back inside with Nero, took him straight to the anaesthetic station where the nurse was waiting with an oxygen mask and the antidote to his sedation. At this stage, the panic was over. I could see that Nero was breathing normally again, and the pink colour had returned to his gums.

My unorthodox procedure had been successful: the centrifugal forces generated by whirling Nero around my head had forced the stone upwards and outwards from his lungs. This wasn't a random procedure that I'd made up on the spur of the moment: it was a technique that I had learned as a vet student when working on a sheep farm. Lambs are often born unable to breathe because their airways are clogged up with fluid and mucus. In a hospital situation, human babies with similar issues are treated with delicate suction apparatus. In an open field, with no medical equipment, the fastest, most-effective way to dispel debris from a lamb's lungs is to hold its back legs, and spin it around. And in the emergency with Nero, this was the only method available to me to remove that small stone from his lungs.

To be extra sure that I'd solved his problem, I took a quick follow up x-ray picture of Nero before he had fully woken up. Sure enough, the small stone was no longer in his lungs. It was only later when Nero was sitting up comfortably in his cage that I went outside to the grassy lawned area surrounded by a concrete path that was my whirling-arena. I didn't think I'd be able to find it, but I had heard the noise when the pebble had hit the clinic wall, so I knew where to hunt. To my surprise, there it was in the middle of the path: a tiny pebble, not much bigger than a frozen pea. I put it into a small clear plastic envelope to show Kath later.

Nero didn't need any follow-up treatment. His cough had been caused directly by the pebble stuck in his airway, so now that it had been removed, the problem was solved. He never coughed again.

I gave Kath the stone, and she looked at it in awe. 'Can I keep it?' she asked. 'Of course,' I replied, 'as long as you don't let him inhale it again.'

Three months later, Nero came back for his annual health check. He sat on my consulting table, staring at me with his usual unforgiving gaze. One of the frustrating parts of the job of a vet is that our patients never appreciate our work on their behalf. Nero was not happy to be in the vet clinic: he would never make the connection between his last visit and his life being saved.

As I looked at him, I noticed that there was a small object dangling from his collar, beside his metal identity disc. When he moved, it tinkled quietly against the metal.

'Is that what I think it is?' I asked Kath.

'I'm afraid so,' she replied. 'I couldn't resist. My hobby is polishing stones to make them into jewellery. That pebble was the perfect size for his collar. I felt that Nero could do with some reminding of how his vet saved his life.'

Of course Nero never realised the significance of his new collar adornment. But the local birds would have appreciated the extra warning caused by its tinkling as he stalked them.

And for Kath and me, whenever Nero came back to my clinic, there was an enjoyable irony that made us both smile. Emperor Nero, carrying around, on public display, the tiny object that nearly brought about his demise.

Questions and answers about pets and foreign objects

Animals' bodies do not react well to the presence of foreign objects. While an inhaled stone, such as Nero suffered, is rare, I've been asked many questions about other situations where external objects have been causing potential problems.

I have long dark hair, and bizarrely, my bearded dragon seems to have a taste for it. On a couple of occasions, I've been leaning over his tank talking to him, and he's reached out with his tongue and tugged a hair out. He's swallowed it before I've been able to stop him. Could this cause a problem?

CD by email

The problem with hair is that it's completely indigestible. In most instances, it'll probably pass through your bearded dragon's digestive tract unhindered, emerging at the other end a few days later. But there's a risk that a strand of hair could get tangled during its passage from the mouth to the rear end. At any point along the way where there are narrower sections in the system, the hair could get caught: the back of the mouth, in the oesophagus, at the exit of the stomach, or in the intestines themselves. This may never happen, but if it did, it would be complicated to get it sorted. It'd be far safer to prevent such potential problems: in future, put on a hair band or net before going near him.

> My three-year-old spayed female cat has always brought things in from the outside, such as leaves and bits of rubbish etc. However, she developed a passion for bringing back gloves, hats, shoes and children's toys from neighbouring properties. I return the items when I know where they've come from, but sometimes I haven't a clue which neighbour she's been visiting. Recently this has become a daily occurrence. How can I deal with my kleptomaniac cat? I also worry that she'll swallow one of the small toys that she steals.
>
> *SF by email*

It sounds as if you'll need to do some detective work. There are now GPS tracking devices that can be attached to your cat via a harness. The most basic version costs £40, and it stores a record of your cat's location. When she returns home, you plug the device into your computer. The information that's downloaded allows you to track exactly where your cat has been on Google Earth. It's also possible to buy a 'live' tracker, which uses mobile phone technology to pinpoint your cat's location at any time of day. A 'cat cam' would give you an even more detailed analysis of her activities. This is a shock-resistant tiny camera that attaches to your cat's collar. Photographs are taken at regular intervals, and when your cat comes home, you can download the images onto your computer and see for yourself exactly where she's been causing mischief.

> Timmy, my four-month-old Jack Russell, often gets hiccoughs. It usually happens after he's eaten. It's very similar to a human with hiccoughs, but with less noise. It last up to twenty minutes then stops. It probably happens twice a week. Why does this happen and can I do anything to prevent it? Could this be caused by something small getting stuck in his airways?
>
> *JW, Manchester*

I've heard of all sorts of animals getting hiccoughs, including dogs, cats, rabbits and even ferrets. Basically, hiccoughs are repeated, involuntary contractions of the diaphragm that cause air to rush into the lungs. As a reflex, the larynx snaps shut, interrupting the inhalation of air, and causing the 'hiccough' sound. Young animals are particularly prone to hiccoughs, probably because they tend to gobble their food more quickly. It's definitely not caused by anything physical causing irritation. To prevent hiccoughs, I've heard about people putting large stones into their dog's bowl so that the dog has to eat more slowly, picking out the food rather than eating it in a rush. You can even buy a dog bowl, with built-in partitions, that forces a dog to eat more slowly. Most pups grow out of hiccoughs, adopting a more dignified style of eating as they mature.

7

Prescription sunglasses for a dog

One of the enjoyable aspect of my job as a vet is the lifelong relationships that I have with my patients. Animals' lives, with their lifespan of just ten to fifteen years, rush past at around seven times the speed of humans', so it's normal for vets to see animals from birth through to the geriatric years. This has its sad side of course, but there's also a sense of satisfaction, of completeness and of rightness: we see life in its entirety, from start to finish.

Shelley was one of my favourite animals. I first met her when she was an eight-week-old wire-haired terrier puppy. Her owner, Mary, was around my age and lived with her elderly mother. She was an exemplary dog owner: she did everything that could possibly be done for Shelley, but did not spoil her. Mary had an almost old-fashioned faith in the opinion of her vet. She didn't go off to Google and come back with her own ideas on what she should do for her pet. When she brought Shelley to see me, she gave me the fullest possible description of what was happening. She kept notebooks with precise timings of any details that might be relevant, from meal times to toileting details to sleeping hours. Then Mary would allow me to examine Shelley carefully, sometimes pointing out minor issues she'd noticed, such as a small bump under the skin, or a slight scratch on one side of her head. Sometimes, a vet needs patience to listen carefully to an owner's detailed description of the minutiae of their pet's daily activities, but this was never the case with Mary. She was an intelligent woman who limited herself to the sharing of relevant details. Yes, there was plenty of information, but it was nearly always useful information that helped me to better understand what might be wrong with Shelley.

And Mary was equally intelligent with the receiving of information. She listened to every word I said, never interrupting. I knew that she was thinking as well as listening, and she'd sometimes go on to ask perceptive questions. She'd also write down the most important aspects of Shelley's recommended treatments to be certain that she'd get everything right. My consultations with Mary and Shelley were always rewarding: I felt that the little dog was getting the best possible care. Shelley lived the typically healthy life of a cross-bred terrier, with no serious illnesses. She had occasional upset stomachs, a couple of minor accidents and a few lumps and bumps that needed simple surgical removal as she grew older. But overall, she was utterly cherished and had the type of life that any dog would long for: a doting owner, ideal living conditions, regular play and exercise and, of course, a vet who saw her as his friend.

It was when she reached the age of thirteen that she developed a peculiar problem that was to baffle us all for some time. By this stage, she had slowed down, only going for walks rather than the energetic runs and chases of her youth. Mary came in to see me, looking anxious. She had her usual notebook in her hand. After greeting Shelley, I asked Mary what was up: Shelley seemed to be in good spirits, but was there something troubling her?

'She's been falling,' Mary told me. 'She'll be walking along normally, then suddenly, her head has been jerking upwards, and she's fallen onto her knees. I wasn't too worried the first time it happened: I thought maybe she'd stood on a stone or something. But she's started to do it regularly.'

Mary then referred to her notebook, and listed the two or three times daily over the previous five days that she'd seen this happen. It seemed to be getting worse. As well as falling, she would twist to her side, snarling and yelping. She would then sit down, looking anxiously at Mary, as if saying, 'That was very unpleasant: please help me!'

Mary's notes confirmed that Shelley was otherwise in good order: eating and drinking normally, with all bodily functions happening regularly.

Mary was worried about her dog. Often, the worst thing is the worry: it's the thought that there might be something sinister and malignant, quietly and insidiously working its course through your pet. That's why Mary was here to see me. She wanted me to reassure her that there was nothing to worry about, or conversely, if her fears were to be realised, she wanted to know the full, awful truth so that she could deal with it.

I examined Shelley carefully all over. She was an aged animal now, with greying fur, stiff joints, and eyes that were beginning to turn misty with early cataracts. But she was fundamentally healthy: her heart was beating regularly and slowly, with no murmurs, her lungs were clear and quiet when I listened to them with my stethoscope, and she had no areas of discomfort or sensitivity when I felt her all over. I did a brief neurological examination, testing the function of her nerves, from the cranial nerves affecting her eyes, ears and face, right through to the nerves emerging from her lower spine, supplying the reflexes of her back legs and the sensation to the tip of her tail. As elsewhere, everything was normal. I could find nothing wrong with Shelley: she was a normal dog, for her age.

'So what's happening then, Pete,' Mary asked me.

I confessed that I really didn't know. There was a long list of possibilities, most of which involved changes to her elderly brain. The only way we could move the diagnostic process forwards would be to carry out advanced diagnostic imaging such as an MRI scan of her skull. And even then, I felt that it was likely that the results would just simply confirm that she did not have the worst conditions that Mary feared, such as brain tumours, haemorrhage or clots. Shelley had absolutely no lingering signs of these issues, such as flicking eyes, absent reflexes or defective areas of sensation. So there was no good indication to carry out such extra tests. My feeling was that the best approach was for Mary to continue to make careful observations about Shelley's behaviour, and we would monitor her progress or deterioration carefully over the coming weeks and months.

Mary brought Shelley back a week later. As soon as I saw the glint in Mary's eye as she came into my consult room, I knew that she had some news for me.

'She's still been having those turns,' she told me, 'but I've worked out what's causing them.'

It was my turn to listen carefully.

'They only happen at a very specific time,' she explained. 'Whenever Shelley steps from the shade into bright sunlight, her head twitches and she starts suddenly, jerking her head upwards, and sometimes stumbling. When I first noticed this, I thought it might have been a coincidence, but I tried it a few times, walking her deliberately from shade into sunlight, and she did it every time.'

It happened to be a sunny evening, so we took Shelley out into the car park, and, staying in a shady area, Mary walked up and down with her on the lead. Once I'd observed her doing this several times uneventfully, Mary moved her towards a sun-dappled area, and walked her straight into the sunlight. As she did this, Shelley's head jerked up, as if she was having some sort of minor transient seizure. Her feet staggered beneath her, and she whined, before gathering herself, and walking on normally.

Mary had successfully identified the inciting cause of Shelley's problem, but the question still remained: why was it happening?

We already knew that Shelley had early cataracts, but could there be some other sort of eye problem leading to increased sunlight sensitivity? I referred Mary to our local veterinary ophthalmologist for a detailed eye examination, using sensitive and powerful equipment.

His report provided our closest possible understanding of what was happening to Shelley. He discovered that she had tiny specks of debris floating inside her eyes. Bright sunlight was causing startling reflections from these specks, and the resulting dazzling glare was upsetting her. She was experiencing a peculiar sensation similar to somebody sneaking up on you and shining an ultra-bright torch light straight into your face. It was no wonder that she was jumping as if startled.

This condition is described in ophthalmology textbooks, and is sometimes known as 'fly-catching', because of the way that dogs bite and snap at the air when they get dazzled.

In the past, there was little that could be done to help cases like this, other than avoiding sunlight. But the specialist mentioned that there was a new product that might help: sunglasses for dogs known as 'Doggles'. These are marketed as a fashion item for dogs, but they also had a genuine function for cases such as Shelley.

I ordered a set of Doggles for Shelley directly from the USA via the company website. Their arrival a week later happened to coincide with Shelley's fourteenth birthday, and so they made the perfect birthday present. They resembled human swimming goggles, attached with an elasticated strap that fitted around the back of her head.

Shelley did not particularly like wearing her Doggles, and she tried to take them off immediately. But she did gradually get used to them, and they did solve her problem. When she was wearing her Doggles, she had no strange episodes at all: she could walk from shade to sunlight without flinching.

The only problem was that Shelley was not a natural sunglasses wearer. She didn't enjoy the sensation of wearing the Doggles, and when Mary let her go off the lead, Shelley would remove them by rubbing her head in the grass.

Mary came up with Shelley's long-term answer: a peaked baseball cap specially designed for a dog. Straps and elastic cords held the cap comfortably and securely in place, and Shelley didn't seem to mind wearing it.

For the rest of her old age, Shelley always wore her cap when out on walks: it became part of her personality. On exceptionally bright sunny days she wore the Doggles as well, but she never seemed to make the connection between wearing these and the extra comfort in sunlight. Passers-by often wondered what this small elderly dog was up to, and Mary became used to explaining that she was a medical patient, not a fashion victim.

Shelley lived till she was sixteen. She eventually developed canine cognitive disorder, which is the dog equivalent of Alzheimer's. It was a long, slow goodbye for Mary, as Shelley gradually stopped being the bright, friendly, engaging dog that she had been. It did mean that when the final farewell eventually happened, we all knew that Shelley was ready. She had enjoyed a wonderful, cherished life, and it was time for her to go on.

She was cremated afterwards, and Mary had three objects that she'd decided to bury with Shelley's ashes in one of her favourite places: her collar, her sunglasses and her baseball cap, which had all been so much a part of her later years.

Questions and answers about pets' visual disturbances

Shelley's extreme reaction to sunlight was rare, but visual distur-
bances in pets are common, and animals can react in unexpected
ways: they can't rationalise that their vision is disturbed because
of an illness. Vets and owners need to be sensitive to the fact that
they can't understand what's happening. Here are some examples
that I've answered in my column.

> We have a rescue Westie, said to be five years old,
> who was thrown out on to the street two years ago.
> He is a lovely dog but he barks incessantly at flashing
> lights on television, as well as thunder and fireworks,
> or any unusual noises. He just will not stop. We would
> be grateful for any suggestions.
>
> *BA, Surrey*

Lots of dogs are afraid of loud noises and light flashes
that resemble lightning or firework flashes. Terriers have a
uniquely confrontational personality, so they tend to bark
at frightening things that would have other dogs hiding
behind the sofa. Since the basis of this problem is fear
of noise, it can be treated in the same way as any fear or
phobia of loud noises. Soundtracks of frightening noises, as

downloadable MP3 files, are available free of charge from the Dog Trust website (www.dogtrust.org.uk). These have been shown to be effective in treating noise phobias such as fireworks, thunder and gunshots. The sounds are played at a low volume, gradually increasing over time, allowing dogs to gradually become accustomed to frightening noises. The reaction to the flashes should be reduced as your dog gradually becomes less afraid of the sounds.

> My Boston terrier, Billy, has eyeballs that are able to move independently of one another. He can watch both me and my boyfriend when we are at opposite sides of the room. Is this normal?
>
> *RM, Bristol*

It sounds as if Billy has 'divergent strabismus', which is the opposite of being cross-eyed. It's an inherited abnormality of the eyeball muscles in Boston terriers and it doesn't mean he can watch you both at the same time: it's just the way his eyes move. If you sit him in front of you, you'll see that his eyes are still both looking to each side. It's a cosmetic issue that won't bother him at all, and nothing needs to be done.

> I am the owner of two cats, a brother and sister. Recently I noticed the female's eyes looked strange,

with the third eyelid in the corner of her eyes showing all the time. Our vet said it was a pollen allergy and gave us eye drops to administer twice a day. Now her brother is showing the same signs. Could there be something more serious going on? What should we do next?

JR by email

Any cat with protruding third eyelids should be checked by a vet to make sure that there's no underlying disease that may not be obvious to an owner. In a one-off case, an allergic reaction is a possibility, but when two cats are affected, other reasons may be more likely. Prominent third eyelids in otherwise healthy cats are sometimes known as 'haws'. The precise cause is often impossible to identify, but it's been reported commonly in cats with mild intestinal disease (e.g. caused by viruses or tapeworms) and in other situations where cats become dehydrated. Once a vet has confirmed that there's nothing else serious happening, time is often the best healer: most cases resolve within a few weeks with no specific treatment.

We have a beautiful miniature schnauzer, aged seven, who has suddenly developed a cataract in her left eye. The other eye seems healthy and normal. We have read that as for a human being, it is possible to have

the cataract removed. How successful are operations
of this kind? Is it worth having the operation done,
given that she has one normal eye that allows her to
see?

JD by email

Cataracts can have a hereditary basis, and if one eye is
affected, there's a risk that the other will go the same way in
due course. Even though the other eye may look normal just
now, the early signs that this is happening can be difficult
to detect without specialised equipment and skills. The eye
is a highly specialised structure, and to work out the best
approach to this situation, you should arrange a referral
to a veterinary ophthalmologist. The operation to remove
cataracts has a success rate of around 95 per cent, but if a
cataract is left in place for too long before the operation,
it can become 'over-mature', which can make it inoperable.
You need to consider the risk that a cataract could develop
in time in the good eye, and if you do nothing, you could
be left wishing that you had resolved the problem in the
first eye. It's well worth arranging at least a preliminary
consultation with a veterinary ophthalmologist as soon as
possible so that you can be given all of the information about
possible options before it's too late.

8

The confident cat with a fear of food

Thor was a well-named large black cross-bred cat. He was so big that he really ought to have been brought to the vet in a dog carrier. Thor occupied so much of a large cat carrier that there was no space for him to stand up or turn around. Once I opened the top-opening carrier, I had to slide one hand down on either side of him, and lift him vertically, as if he was an appliance.

As well as being large and muscular, Thor was confident. Once he was out of his carrier, he would sit on the consulting table and eyeball me, as if considering what he was going to do with me. He was never grumpy or aggressive, but I always felt that he only tolerated me after careful consideration, and that perhaps one day, he might change his mind. I didn't look forward to that day. His owner Sophie had told me how he ruled the local neighbourhood cats: if any of them came into his garden, he'd see them off, and he had a favourite perch on the garden wall from which he used to survey his kingdom. No cats dared to come near to him, and Thor liked it that way.

On this occasion, Sophie was perplexed. Thor had started to behave strangely.

'I'll swear that he has developed a phobia of his food bowl,' she told me. 'At meal times, he has started to back away from it, as if he's frightened it's going to attack him. He still eats if I feed him tasty bits of chicken in a saucer, so I don't think he's ill, but what on earth is going on? Could he be hallucinating after sniffing too much cat-nip? He loves rolling in the plant that grows all over our garden.'

It did seem strange that such a strong, assertive cat could be nervous of an inanimate object. To help me appreciate what was going on, Sophie had a taken a short video on her phone of Thor interacting with his food bowl, and it was just as she said. His pupils dilated, his ears flattened, and he backed away from the bowl, hissing and growling.

'That's just how he starts out with local cats,' she told me, 'except that then he always attacks them and they run away. So far he hasn't attacked his bowl, but maybe that's coming next unless I can get him over this delusion.'

As I looked at Thor on the consulting table, he seemed neither deluded nor frightened. He adopted his usual seated stance, steadily gazing at me. If cats could chew gum, he'd be doing it.

Although I could tell just by looking at him that he was not in some sort of hallucinatory state, I decided to carry out some simple tests to check the functioning of his nervous system. Cats can suffer from a range of brain and other central nervous disorders, and a neurological examination is the best way to get a baseline view of what's going on.

I took him through the standard checklist of nerve-function tests and reflexes. He had full sensation over his entire body (his whiskers twitched whenever I tickled any part of his large frame with tweezers). He was able to walk normally (although it was difficult to make him do this: he just wanted to sit). He had normal reflexes (he stared at me even harder than usual when I used a small rubber hammer to tap below his knees and ankles). His vision and hearing were normal (his gaze followed a small cotton ball held by forceps when I moved it in front of him, and when I crinkled a plastic bag behind him, his ears twitched and he glanced over his shoulder).

I then moved on to a detailed physical examination, and he passed easily. His heart was slow, strong and regular, and his breathing was easy and relaxed. He had no painful or swollen area as I carefully palpated him all over.

The final part of my examination was to inspect Thor's mouth. I asked Sophie to put both hands around his body to steady him, while I put my right hand over his head, grasping one side of his face with my forefinger, and the other with my thumb. I then tilted his head back, which caused his lower jaw to fall open, giving me a good view of his mouth and teeth. As I did this, I could feel Thor's gaze boring into me. I had a sense he was not going to tolerate this much longer, but that didn't matter. I could see the cause of Thor's fear immediately: he had a dramatic neck lesion on his left lower molar tooth.

A neck lesion is the most common form of cat dental disease. Known technically as 'feline odontoclastic resorption lesions'(FORLS), neck lesions are the cat equivalent of human dental decay. These are usually found on the outside of the tooth where the gum meets the tooth surface, especially on the back teeth. The cause is unknown, and there are various theories including an autoimmune response, a viral infection, and metabolic imbalances linked to calcium regulation. As with dental decay in humans, the protective enamel layer of the tooth is eroded, exposing first the underlying dentin and then opening into the exquisitely sensitive pulp canal. This causes toothache that becomes excruciating sharp pain when pressure is applied to the eroded area. In cats, this type of pain often occurs when they attempt to eat dry biscuits.

Now we knew why Thor was frightened of his food bowl. He had tried eating biscuits in the bowl, and the resulting pain in his mouth was the equivalent of him receiving an electric shock. Clearly, soft chicken meat from a saucer did not impact on the sensitive area in the same way.

In the past, vets tried to fix neck lesions by using dental fillings, in the same way as dental decay is treated in humans. Experience showed that these just fell out. So these days, the answer is complete extraction of the affected tooth. The pain is removed, along with the tooth, and modern cats are able to function normally even if they have many teeth extracted. A pain-free mouth is far more important than the ability to chew: modern pet food can be prepared to make it so soft that healthy gums are all that's needed to chew it enough for swallowing.

I admitted Thor to our clinic for the day, and under general anaesthesia, I first took a series of intra-oral x-ray pictures of all his teeth. These showed that he had four teeth affected by neck lesions, so they all needed to be extracted. This complex process was done by using a mini-circular saw to cut each tooth into manageable fragments before removing them. Thor was given a powerful cocktail of pain relief before being sent home that evening.

Sophie called me the next day with good news. 'Not only has Thor lost his fear of his food bowl, but he's fallen in love with it. He scoffed his entire breakfast this morning, and he's now snoozing with his head resting in his food bowl. You definitely hit the right spot with your diagnosis!'

Questions and answers on dental issues in pets

Dental disease, like Nero's, is one of those issues that's often felt acutely by pets, yet is unnoticed by owners: it's so easy for the teeth to hide in a pet's closed mouth. Here are some other cases of tooth-related problems that readers have asked me about in my column.

My two-year-old female rabbit has a tooth problem. Every four weeks she needs to have her bottom front teeth trimmed as these grow forward. The vet has suggested that she has her front two upper and lower teeth removed. The monthly visits are stressful for her but I am concerned that if she has the teeth removed, she may not be able to eat, groom and live her normal carefree life.

SH, Poole

Rabbits' teeth continue to grow throughout their lives. Normally, they are kept short by being naturally filed down by the teeth on the opposite jaw. Your rabbit suffers from 'malocclusion', which means that her upper and lower incisors (front teeth) are not lined up against each other, allowing them unconstrained, continual growth. No one has invented braces to re-align rabbit teeth yet, so regular clipping has been the traditional treatment. In recent years, vets have discovered that full extraction of the incisor teeth is a much better option. It provides a full, permanent cure, with no visible adverse effects. Remember that your rabbit is not able to use her front teeth effectively at the moment anyway, because they do not meet properly. Go ahead and get those front teeth extracted.

> I love taking photos of my hamster, Midas. He looks so cute, especially when he eats small treats, holding them in his paws like a little human. I've noticed that his teeth are a dirty brown/yellow colour. I can use Photoshop to make them whiter, but I wonder if anything can be done for him in real life. Could a vet clean a hamster's teeth? Is bleaching possible for animals?
>
> *CP, Norwich*

Cosmetic dentistry isn't justifiable in the animal world. Pets don't care how white their teeth are, and it wouldn't be fair to put them through any type of uncomfortable procedure just for our own viewing pleasure. Vets often clean dogs' and cats' teeth, but that's because tartar builds up that causes periodontal disease, a problem that small mammals like hamsters don't suffer from. As long as his teeth aren't overgrown or crooked, Midas doesn't need any dental attention: just keep working on your Photoshop skills.

My cat broke his upper canine tooth two years ago and had to have it extracted. Do you think a dental implant would be necessary? I would also like to know if this is a painful procedure and if it is expensive.

EC by email

I'm afraid dental implants are not available for cats anywhere in the world, to my knowledge. The bone volume in a cat's jaw is so small that it would be technically very challenging, and anyway, there's very rarely a need for a tooth to be replaced. It's common for cats to have missing teeth, and they nearly always manage to live normal lives with no adverse consequences, hunting and even eating hard dried food as before. I've seen cats that have had to have all of their teeth extracted, and there's been no significant impact on their daily lives. It's true that in a small proportion of cases, loss of the upper canine tooth in a cat can lead to the lower canine tooth catching the upper lip, causing an abrasion. If this is happening, there are other ways of dealing with this that your vet will be able to explain to you. Dental implants have been done in dogs, but they cost over £5,000 each.

I have a ten-month-old Norfolk terrier bitch whose baby canine teeth have not fallen out. The adult teeth have come now, so she has four teeth, two on each side of her lower jaw. The 'babies' are still firmly in place. Should I take her to the vet and have the 'babies' removed or can I leave them alone?

JB by email

This is a common problem in small breeds of dog. The deciduous ('baby') teeth are meant to be pushed out by the adult teeth when they grow in. If this doesn't happen, the deciduous teeth may remain in place for the whole life of the pet, causing the adult teeth to move into an abnormal position. Pockets and grooves are created between the extra teeth, and these accumulate food and debris, which leads to halitosis, gingivitis and other dental issues. If the deciduous teeth have not fallen out by ten months of age, they're unlikely to do so. For the sake of your dog's oral health, you should talk to your vet about getting them extracted.

9

The truth about practice cats

Ever since I set up my own business as a vet, I have attracted an unusual type of follower: a so-called 'practice cat'. Although this sounds like an animal that a novice veterinarian might acquire to test their surgical skills from time to time, the less-shocking reality is that a vet clinic acts as a magnet to independent cats in an area. Word soon gets around the local feline fraternity that there are friendly people in the vet clinic building. Curious cats start to hang around the doors, and before we know it, the cats adopt the vets.

Our first practice cat was a large assertive black-and-white tom-cat called Tom. He started by waiting outside our kitchen door, slipping indoors when somebody stepped outside to smoke a cigarette. He'd then sidle up to vet nurses during their tea breaks, and he was soon being fed tasty treats in the staff common room. Before long, he had found the cosiest spot in our clinic: a space on the reception desk just above the two computer monitors that generated a pleasant warmth. Our receptionist offered him a cushion to lie on here, and this became his favoured sleeping space. He woke up occasionally when the waiting room was busy, surveying an audience of people and dogs through half-open eyes. But mostly he slept, saving himself for the nights out and about in the neighbourhood. Tom was the ideal conversation piece for a veterinary waiting room, with people sometimes wondering if this stationary sleeping body was a real, live cat. He had one bad habit: he occasionally took a dislike to a customer, and randomly lashed out with a front foot. He never hurt anyone, but he gave a few people a fright, and understandably, there were intermittent calls for Tom to be banned from the waiting room. He was an independent creature who refused to be confined indoors, insisting on heading out on his own every evening when the clinic closed. We worried about him, but that's how he wanted to live his life. He had an adventurous, risk-taking personality and, eventually, he suffered the consequences. We were devastated when we came to work one morning to discover that he'd been struck by a passing car outside our clinic and had died instantly. Tom was cremated, and his ashes returned to us in a carved wooden casket in the shape of a sleeping cat.

In his memory, a carved cat has been placed in Tom's former sleeping place at our reception desk, just as Tom might have liked.

Soon after Tom died, another cat turned up: a large tabby cat who was named Caleb by one of our nurses. Caleb preferred to stay behind the scenes, which was welcomed after Tom's questionable waiting room behaviour. Caleb somehow negotiated a cushion in an open kitchen cupboard, and he slept there all day. He always enjoyed his food, and whenever there was activity in the staff common room, he'd purr as he moved from person to person, entreating everyone to offer him the tastiest parts of their sandwiches. When Caleb had been living with us for three years, he brought a young female tabby cat back with him after a night's adventuring. She just turned up one morning, and he seemed to enjoy her presence. He even allowed her to sleep close to him (obviously, he kept the prime cushioned sleeping area for himself). This new cat was named Girlfriend, because it was clear to everyone that Caleb had found himself a girlfriend.

As residential cats, Caleb and Girlfriend have been cherished. They've been vaccinated, wormed, treated for fleas, microchipped and neutered. They have regular check-ups, and anything amiss is spotted promptly by one of the dozen vets and nurses who encounter the two cats every day. They have optimal, self-selected nutrition. Over the years, they have been offered a range of products, but if they have ever been given something they dislike, they express their discontent very clearly. Equally, they have been known to walk in to our food store and open their desired bag with a quick slash of their sharp front claws.

They're both elderly animals now. Caleb had his twentieth birthday early this year, and Girlfriend is not far behind at sixteen. A few years ago, they chose a new sleeping area in a small office that had been used as our 'fax and photocopying room'. The warm room isn't used that often in this email and internet age, so the cats tend to be left in peace. They started to sleep on cushions near the warm electronic equipment, and the room increasingly became their territory. They stopped going out so often, and we introduced litter trays and feed bowls for them. As they became less active outside, we brought in cat scratch posts and toys to entertain them. These days they are indoor-only cats, only emerging for occasional forays among the staff in the common room, looking for extra food treats.

They've been healthy animals, but they had one major health scare, a few years ago. Caleb was sixteen when one of his toes became swollen, and he started to hobble around. Given his age, we were worried about the possibility of cancer, so moved him into our cat ward for a work up. We collected blood and urine samples, he was sedated and x-rayed, and we started treatment with potent antibiotics and pain relief. Thankfully, the test results were all normal, and after three days of treatment, his toe returned to a normal size. It had just been a bacterial infection, perhaps started by a minor puncture wound.

While Caleb was being treated, an issue developed with Girlfriend. First, she refused to eat (and she loved her food, so this was serious). Then she started to yowl loudly, several times a day. Again, this was completely out of character. And she looked unkempt and disgruntled. Something was definitely amiss.

We started Girlfriend's work up by taking blood and urine samples: everything was normal. We then measured her blood pressure. High blood pressure is common in older cats, and is often linked with serious ailments like kidney failure and heart disease. When the blood pressure is too high, consequences include brain haemorrhages and sudden blindness from bleeding at the back of the eye.

Blood pressure is measured in a similar way to humans, using a wrap-around tourniquet on the foreleg, listening to blood flow starting and stopping with a special electronic stethoscope. Girlfriend yowled loudly as we did this, and the results were clear: her blood pressure was 50 per cent higher than it should be. She needed immediate medication to change the dynamics of blood flow around her body, to bring the pressure down as soon as possible. We decided that she should stay in the cat ward while this was given, so that we could watch her closely.

As I carried her through the ward to the cage that had been prepared for her, we passed Caleb in his cage. He was recovering from sedation, and he sleepily lifted his head to look at us. Girlfriend let out another of her loud miaows, and I had a sudden thought. Instead of taking her to her own cage, I moved her bed to Caleb's cage, and put her in with him. She went straight up to him, licking behind his ears, then moved over to curl up comfortably in her bed, which I had placed beside him.

On a whim, I decided to measure Girlfriend's blood pressure again, with her staying exactly where she was, still in her bed close to Caleb. I had to take the measurements three times, because I didn't believe the results at first. Her blood pressure had returned completely to normal.

The cause of her 'illness' seemed obvious now. I offered her some of the food that she had refused earlier, and she tucked into it hungrily. She then sat up and groomed herself thoroughly, nibbling out the tiny knots and mats from her fur. When I went back to see her an hour later, she no longer looked unkempt, and she was purring.

Sometimes the answer to veterinary mysteries is far more obvious than the investigating vets would like to think. Science and technology can blind us to simple facts that are in full sight.

Girlfriend had been missing her boyfriend.

Questions and answers on pets in old age

Few animals reach the age of twenty or more, but the average life span of pets is increasing, and I'm often asked questions about issues relating to old age. Here are some questions that I've answered about geriatric pets in my column.

We are thinking of relocating to the south of Spain. We would be taking our two toy poodles with us, one aged eleven, the other aged fifteen. The fifteen-year-old suffers from cataracts and is almost blind. We've been told (not by vets) that the hot summers would be too much for them and that they would be unlikely to survive. What would be your thoughts on this?

RF by email

There are plenty of geriatric dogs living happily in the south of Spain, and I find it hard to understand why somebody thinks that your dogs would be 'unlikely to survive'. Of course, you'd need to take special care of them, making sure that they aren't exposed to undue heat stress, but in this age of widespread air conditioning, that shouldn't be too difficult. You should make an appointment with your vet before you go, ·to talk about the various health issues that are common in Mediterranean areas, such as heart worm. Such illnesses can easily be prevented by regular medication, but it's best to know about what you need to do before you leave.

> Over the last five years, my twelve-year-old collie's thick black coat has gradually changed to a lighter shade of auburn. Could she be lacking some essential ingredient in her diet?
>
> *NB, Co Down*

In theory, a dietary mineral deficiency could affect coat colour, but if she is fed on commercial pet food, this will not be the case. The three most likely causes are old age (just as humans turn grey, some pets go a lighter colour), an underlying hormonal disease (but you'd expect other signs, such as an increased thirst, weight gain or bald areas) or exposure to sunlight (many pets turn a lighter colour in summer months or warmer climates).

> My eighteen-year-old female cat has always kept her coat in pristine condition. She is short haired, and I comb her every day, but recently I've noticed thick clumps in her fur at the rear end. I have tried to separate by teasing them out but she does not like this. If left will these grow out? Is this an age-related problem or a sign of an underlying complaint?
>
> *PD, Worcestershire*

Matted fur on the lower back is common in older cats, and can happen for a number of reasons, including lack of flexibility due to arthritis, dental disease preventing thorough self-grooming, and general geriatric lethargy. Ideally, early intervention can solve this, by gently teasing out the clumped fur before it accumulates. If you leave the clumps alone, they will get bigger, forming uncomfortable pads of matted fur. The best answer is to ask your vet to remove the clumped areas with electric clippers: during the same visit, you can ask about any related issues that your cat may need help with, such as dental disease, arthritis and other hidden geriatric problems that can often be helped with simple treatment.

Our eleven-year-old large grey rabbit has started putting his head down on the floor of the hutch quite often. He can still get around the garden and is eating well. His teeth have been inspected this year and are OK. Is this normal behaviour in old age?

CK, Hants

Your rabbit is the equivalent of an octogenarian human. It's not 'normal' for any rabbit to behave as you describe, but it's probably 'normal' for old rabbits to behave in unusual ways. You need to get a vet to make sure that there is not a serious reason for this odd behaviour. It's great that you get his teeth checked regularly, but a more frequent veterinary check-up is very useful for all geriatric animals – including rabbits – if they are not in glorious good health. A more frequent visit to the vet e.g. every three months can often pick up early changes caused by disease (such as minor weight loss) before the situation has become too advanced. Rabbits can be very good at covering up underlying illnesses, so they need to be physically checked even more carefully than dogs or cats.

10

The travelling parasite

At seven years of age, Ted was a healthy beagle: as fit and strong as any dog. Renata had owned him since he was a puppy, having bought him from a breeder in her native Warsaw, in Poland. When she decided to move to Ireland, there was no question about it: Ted was coming with her. Renata planned the journey carefully, using a professional animal transportation company to make sure that everything went smoothly. Ted was microchipped, vaccinated against rabies, issued with the standard European Pet Passport and given a compulsory comprehensive worm dose before leaving Poland, to prevent accidentally importing rare dog worms that could affect the Irish dog population. Renata also placed an anti-flea-and-tick collar around Ted's neck: this wasn't a legal stipulation but she wanted to ensure that he would have a healthy, hassle-free start to his new life in Ireland. The journey from Poland to Ireland went smoothly. Ted was a good traveller, even seeming to enjoy the combination of car and ferry journeys.

Two days after their arrival, Renata discovered a large blood-filled tick on Ted's lower body. She knew that while ticks are usually harmless, they can carry diseases that can affect humans as well as dogs, so she wore plastic gloves as she carefully plucked it off him, making sure that she didn't break off the tick's head as she did so. Abscesses and wound reactions are common if ticks are carelessly removed. She then threw the tick into a fire, ensuring that it was safely and completely destroyed.

Three days after Ted's arrival in Ireland, he refused to get out of his bed. He didn't want to eat his breakfast, and he looked miserable. This was such a dramatic change from normal that Renata knew something was seriously wrong. She took Ted to the nearest vet who identified at once that he had a high temperature. Just as in humans, dogs with high temperatures become quiet, sleepy, unwilling to move and lose their appetites. Sometimes the underlying cause of a high temperature is a bacterial or a viral infection, and there's a long list of other possible causes, from rare cancers to auto-immune disorders. There was no obvious cause of the high temperature in Ted's case. He seemed in good condition physically, apart from his general malaise. The vet decided to give him a course of broad-spectrum antibiotics, which would effectively treat most underlying bacterial infections. If he failed to make a full recovery, more detailed investigations would be needed. Vets are acutely aware that routine investigations – such as blood samples, x-rays and ultrasound – can be expensive, so they are often only done if an animal has not responded to an initial general treatment.

Ted did seem to improve at first, brightening up and beginning to eat, but a week later he was dull and lethargic again, and he'd stopped eating completely, so Renata brought him to see me. She explained Ted's complicated story, and I examined the little dog, not expecting to find anything dramatic.

I carried out my usual physical clinical examination, and as well as still having a high temperature, Ted had two other significant abnormalities. First, his heart was racing. A dog's pulse is normally around 100 to 130 beats per minute. Ted's pulse was pitter-pattering along at 200 beats per minute.

Second, when I lifted Ted's lips and examined the colour of his gums, they were far too pale. The gums should have a deep pink colour: in Ted's case they were closer to white than pink.

The combination of rapid heart and pale gums was typical of anaemia, when a dog has a low blood count. I took a blood sample, and processed it immediately in our in-house laboratory. The result confirmed my suspicions: Ted had around half the normal level of red blood cells. He was definitely anaemic, but the question remained: why?

There are three broad causes of anaemia. First, blood loss: if an animal loses blood after an accident, anaemia follows. This was not the case with Ted: there had been no sign of any bleeding, and there had been no possibility of any type of trauma.

The second cause of anaemia is reduced red blood cell production. There's a continual natural wastage of blood cells, as part of the body's daily wear and tear. If the body stops producing red blood cells, there's a slow reduction in the blood count as the population of cells gradually gets used up. Red blood cells are produced by the bone marrow, and a wide range of causes – from toxins to cancer – can stop this production. Ted's background didn't make this cause of anaemia likely: his problem seemed to have developed too rapidly.

The third cause of anaemia – and the most likely one in Ted's case – was that something was destroying his red blood cells as they circulated. The most common cause of this is an auto-immune disease, where the body's immune system starts to attack a dog's own red blood cells. While this was a possibility, after listening to the story of Ted's unusual background, I'd worked out that there was a more likely explanation in his case.

I examined a drop of his blood under a high-powered microscope and found exactly what I was looking for. Ted's red blood cells could be seen as small pale red circles, the normal appearance. But some of his red blood cells contained pairs of small oval purple shapes, like tiny elongated cherries. While I had never seen anything like this under a microscope before, thanks to a dim memory from my veterinary student days, I knew exactly what they were: a Polish blood parasite called *Babesia canis*, which Ted had picked up from his tick infestation. We don't have that tick in Ireland or the UK, but whenever an animal is imported from another country, the list of possible illnesses has to be extended to include conditions that could have been picked up elsewhere.

I now had enough information to be able to treat Ted, but to be certain of the diagnosis, I sent off a blood sample to a commercial laboratory for so-called polymerase chain reaction (PCR) analysis. This is a molecular biological technique that uses enzymes to amplify small quantities of DNA to create a larger volume of DNA that allows for a very specific and precise diagnosis of the type of blood parasite that I'd found.

While we waited for that detailed result, thousands of tiny *Babesia* organisms were currently destroying Ted's red blood cells. He needed urgent life-saving treatment, which was not easy to find since there is no licensed product in this country to treat this exotic illness in dogs. I phoned around some of my farm veterinary colleagues, and eventually tracked down a cattle product that would be effective. Cows in Ireland often suffer from a different form of babesiosis known as redwater, so farm vets need the drug that kills this type of parasite. The product isn't licensed for dogs, but if I didn't do something quickly, Ted was going to die. I telephoned the product manufacturer to confirm that it would be safe to use, and once I had their agreement, I drew up a dog-sized dose – just one-fifth of a teaspoonful – in a syringe and injected it directly into the vein in Ted's foreleg.

Ted had to stay on an intravenous drip in our veterinary hospital, being hand-fed, for another couple of days. Some anaemic dogs need a blood transfusion to keep them alive, but Ted was lucky not to be so severely affected. As the anti-babesia medication took effect, his temperature returned to normal and he started to feel hungry. His blood count began to increase, his interest in life returned, and he was visibly getting better. I sent him home as soon as he was eating proper meals, and he continued to improve day by day.

By the time he came back to see me for a check-up a week later, the final laboratory results had returned, with the DNA analysis confirming that the cause of his anaemia was *Babesia canis*.

A repeat blood test confirmed that his anaemia had almost fully resolved. Renata told me that Ted was completely back to normal, wanting to play with his toys, and even begging for food. Renata would normally discourage him from begging: it's an annoying bad habit. But just for this week of Ted's life, she encouraged him. It was just such a relief to see Ted's normal enthusiasm for life and food restored: how could she ever say no to him again?

Questions and answers on external parasites (ticks, mites and fleas)

External parasites – such as ticks – commonly affect household pets, although life-threatening consequences like Ted's crisis are rare. Here are some of the queries about ticks, mites and fleas that I've answered in the past.

> Every summer, we go on a family holiday in late August to a cottage in the Scottish Highlands. We go on long walks across moors and glens, and our five-year-old golden retriever Susie just loves these. The only problem is that she always ends up getting ticks on her body and her head. I never know what to do about these. Should I rush to the vet (as I have done in the past) or should I try to remove them myself with a lighted cigarette (as one of the locals up there told me to do)?
>
> *BW, Edinburgh*

Ticks can be annoying for dogs, and they can (rarely) carry disease, so it is best to remove them. You need to do this carefully, since if the tick's head breaks off in the dog, it can cause a nasty reaction. There are many old wives' tales about how to remove ticks, but most of them don't work very well. The easiest, safest way to remove a tick is with a special plastic tick-removing tool, known as the O'Tom Tick Remover. You can buy these at many vet clinics, and it is probably best to have a demonstration on its use for the first time. A video and explanation of its use can also be seen online at www.otom.com.

> Despite treating our dogs with spot-on products containing fipronil, they are constantly picking up ticks. Today she had three new ones on her head and I found an engorged one on the kitchen floor. I am losing faith with the commercially available products. What can I do?
>
> *SK, Oxfordshire*

Fipronil is only one of over a dozen safe modern chemicals that are available to prevent and kill ticks, and as well as spot-on products, you can use oral tablets, sprays, oral formulations and impregnated collars. Some products are licensed to repel ticks whereas others work only by killing ticks once they have attached to your dog. The most recently developed, potent products are often released first through vets, on a prescription-only basis, so the best answer is to visit your local vet with a specific question: 'Can you supply me with the most effective type of tick control?' Ticks can be challenging to prevent completely, so whatever product you choose, you should still check for occasional ticks, and remove them.

Our neutered male cat has patchy baldness around the base of his tail. This happened last year and our vet said this was due to fleas (although we could not find any on him). He got worse despite expensive treatment for fleas, but then his fur grew in during the winter. What could be going on?

SV by email

The tail head is a classic focus for flea irritation, but the fleas often remain invisible. Up to 70 per cent of itchy cats referred to skin specialists make a full recovery simply by using thorough flea control, even when no fleas have been seen. It's warm enough for fleas to breed outside in the summer, but too cold for them in the winter. If your cat visits flea-rich outdoor areas in the summer, this can be a challenge for many flea treatments, since the fleas may need to nibble a treated cat before they are killed. Ask your vet about alternative, more rapidly acting, flea control.

My one-year-old budgie has a beak problem: it has lost its normal smooth shiny shape, and has gone dull and rough-looking. It doesn't seem serious enough to go the vet, but I'm worried about it. What should I do?

ED, London

Budgies are prone to a microscopic mite, known as the Scaly beak mite, or *Cnemidocoptes* (see chapter 22). It can also affect the legs, causing thickening and scaliness around the feet. It is a potentially serious problem: it's highly infectious between budgies and I have even seen one bird losing its beak because its owner delayed seeking treatment for too long. Pet shops sell lotions and creams that may help, but the definitive answer is a one-off visit to your vet. The diagnosis of mites can be confirmed by examining a sample under the microscope. A single application of a prescription-only anti-parasite drop is usually effective at killing the mite, and your budgie's beak should rapidly return to normal.

11

The terrier with a tumour that wouldn't go away

Cancer. Some words carry such negative connotations that once spoken people's thought processes freeze, and the rest of the sentence is sometimes not even heard. As a vet in practice, I try to avoid using that word. There are other, more accurate and appropriate words that can make it easier for people to understand what's happening with their pets. My own preferred word is 'tumour': a tumour can be benign – or harmless – or it can be malignant. A malignant tumour somehow feels more precise and narrowly defined. Cancer seems to be a large black amorphous cloud, like a malevolent octopus squirting murky ink around. A malignant tumour feels more solid and tangible, more likely to be captured and confined. Of course, the sad truth is that whatever word is used, the disease that is cancer is still one of our biggest challenges. The diagnosis and treatment of malignant tumours is something that vets have to deal with every week. Despite our best efforts, cancer often – but not always – wins.

Pooch was an active middle-aged Jack Russell terrier who lived life at top speed. She was a petite, fine-boned creature, with the dappled brown-and-white coat markings typical of her breed. When Geraldine noticed that her left elbow had a small blister-like swelling, she presumed Pooch had bashed it in her mad dashing around but she was not too worried. She brought the little dog in to see me just to be safe.

When first I examined Pooch, I was not too worried either. The swelling was tiny and soft, like a small water-filled balloon. It's common for active dogs to sprain or bruise their joints during boisterous exercise, and that seemed the most likely cause. To rule out other possibilities, I collected a small sample of the fluid with a sterile syringe and needle. Pooch barely noticed – one of the joys of being a dog is their continual sense of living in the moment. While neither Geraldine nor I had serious concerns, Pooch had none at all. She knew her evening walk was due, and this knowledge filled her with delight. I sent the sample off to the laboratory for analysis, which I hoped would back up my opinion. Meanwhile, I gave Pooch some anti-inflammatory medication, and asked Geraldine to limit her to lead-only exercise for a few days. I fully expected that the swelling would rapidly resolve.

The laboratory result seemed to confirm my clinical impression. The cells were suggestive of an accumulation of joint fluid due to trauma such as a sprain. There was no evidence of anything more complicated, such as infection or tumour cells. When I phoned Geraldine to pass on the good news, I was surprised to hear the swelling was worse, and Pooch was now limping.

This would not be expected with a simple sprain. It was time to investigate further, so Pooch was booked in for x-ray pictures. These first x-rays didn't show anything dramatically wrong. There were signs of arthritis around her elbow, common in a middle-aged dog, and the swelling was now twice as big as it had been the first day, so I drained the fluid again, bandaged her leg, and sent her home on anti-inflammatory medication for another week. The laboratory findings had reassured me that there was no hint of anything other than a sprain: perhaps she just needed stricter rest, and stronger medication to take away the inflammation.

Much to the little dog's frustration (she loved her walks), Geraldine rested Pooch strictly, but a week later, my treatment had failed. The lameness was worse and the blister had swelled up again. This apparently simple problem was becoming worrying. While there was no evidence of anything sinister, the condition wasn't behaving as expected for a simple, benign ailment.

Further investigation was needed so this time I arranged

an ultrasound examination. Ultrasound scanning is like radar on a tiny scale. Its best-known use is to look at babies in the womb, but the technique is useful whenever a three-dimensional real-time view is needed of almost anything in the body. Ultrasound can be done on a conscious animal: fur is clipped away from the area to be examined, and a smooth probe is placed on the skin's surface. Ultrasonic soundwaves are beamed out from the probe, and the echo is then received by the probe. Different body tissues have varying levels of sound-wave reflectivity, and computer algorithms are used to create a three-dimensional image that represents the internal body structures.

The initial ultrasound scan gave me the first evidence that something was seriously wrong with Pooch's elbow. A large area of abnormal tissue in the muscle beside her elbow was identified; its 3cm diameter was substantial in a small terrier dog. I sedated Pooch and took a sample of the abnormal tissue, using a technique known as a 'fine needle aspirate': under ultrasound guidance, a fine needle was pushed into the abnormal area, and cells were collected for laboratory analysis.

At this stage, I knew that we were in challenging territory: it was now most likely that the abnormal tissue was some type of malignant tumour, although other diseases, such as rare fungal infections, could cause similar findings. I shared my suspicions with Geraldine, but it was very important to be 100 per cent sure. If Pooch had a malignant tumour around her elbow, she would have to have her left foreleg amputated. This is a radical, life-changing procedure, and not something to be done lightly. It would be lamentable to remove Pooch's leg and subsequently discover her problem could have been cured with anti-fungal medication.

I expected the laboratory analysis of the needle aspirate to confirm the presence of cancer cells, giving us a clear rationale to proceed with amputation of Pooch's leg. Instead, although the pathologist identified abnormal cells, he was not able to identify them precisely and requested that we take a full biopsy. A fine needle aspirate sample is like a few crumbs from the middle of a loaf of bread. In most cases, this is enough to make a clear diagnosis of the nature of a tumour. Sometimes, however, a full biopsy – the equivalent of a chunk of bread rather than just crumbs – is needed to gain a clear understanding of the identity of abnormal tissue.

Pooch needed a general anaesthetic for the biopsy to be taken. A surgical instrument like a mini apple corer was pushed into the diseased area to collect a cylindrical core of abnormal tissue. Again, I used ultrasound to make sure that the sample was collected from the middle of the diseased area. I was confident that this time the laboratory would give us a confirmed diagnosis of the type of malignant tumour, but again, the results were frustratingly inconclusive. The biopsy was definitely abnormal, but it was simply not possible to clearly define the type of abnormality. I still had a strong 'gut feeling' that Pooch had cancer of her elbow, and the correct treatment was amputation of her leg. But without the laboratory results to back up the diagnosis, I could not justify going ahead.

I phoned the laboratory for a one-to-one conversation with the pathologist. I knew him well: one of the pleasures of the veterinary world is that it's small, and we often know one another. I had worked in Africa with Tim when we were both new graduates, so it was easy to have a frank discussion.

I pleaded with him: 'Tim, surely you can tell from the biopsy? We just need to know. Can't you have another look and find an answer for me?' Of course, even for a friend, Tim couldn't change what he saw. The only answer was to try again, with a fresh sample. Despite strong clinical impressions, a diagnosis of a malignant tumour – of cancer – can only be made when definitive evidence is seen by a pathologist. Until then, we just could not be sure, and so we could not treat her with confidence.

The next day, under sedation, I took another sample of fluid from the swelling. Perhaps the disease would have advanced enough to give me a different result this time. Again, the results from Tim were inconclusive. It was very frustrating for everyone, especially Pooch, who was now very lame, with an elbow that was more swollen than ever.

The only way to solve puzzles like this is to keep trying. I could have taken an MRI scan, but this would simply have shown us the abnormal area, as we had seen on the ultrasound. Instead, I anaesthetised Pooch once more, and repeated the x-rays. These now showed that the bone around her elbow was beginning to be eroded by sinister darkened patches of bone destruction. This provided supplementary evidence: a malignant tumour was the only disease likely to behave like this. Yet, it was still not definitive; we needed the equivalent of a DNA match to be certain. The only way to prove my suspected diagnosis was to collect a sample that allowed Tim to identify malignant cells. I trusted his ability completely: the only villain in this piece was the malignant tumour itself.

I took yet another sample of fluid from the swelling. This time, at last, Tim was able to make a clear diagnosis. This sample contained well-defined malignant cells. The type of cancer was invasive and aggressive, so invasive that it would be impossible to dissect it out, and other treatment modalities like radiation treatment and chemotherapy would be futile. The only hope was to cut it out leaving a wide margin of healthy tissue between Pooch's body and the cancer. That meant that the treatment needed for Pooch was to amputate her front left leg at the shoulder.

The investigation of Pooch's problem had been long-winded and had tested everyone's patience, but at least we now knew the truth, and we knew what we had to do to save her life.

Her operation went well, and within a few days, Pooch was adapting to life on three legs. Within a month, she was running around as nimbly as if she still had four legs. Dogs manage remarkably well in these situations: a dog with a missing leg can live a normal life in nearly every way, just as a three-legged stool is almost as stable as a four-legged chair.

The tumour had been fully and thoroughly excised, and now that the limb had been amputated, I was able to give Tim the most comprehensive tissue sample possible, for full analysis. I sent him Pooch's entire elbow, pickled in formalin. He was able to take multiple slices, with different angulations and from different perspectives, using a range of stains. This detailed histopathological analysis confirmed that the tumour had been a 'histiocytic sarcoma', a malignancy that is notoriously difficult to diagnose and treat. Tim's report told me that there was a serious possibility that the tumour might recur, despite Pooch's radical amputation. Some malignant tumours send out packages of malignant cells, similar to that metaphorical octopus with its cloud of ink. It would be possible to refer Pooch to a specialist centre for radiation treatment, but by now, Geraldine and her family felt that Pooch had been through enough. She was enjoying her walks again, loving life on three legs, and their view was that enough was enough. What would be, would be.

I'd love to write that Pooch lived for another seven years, dying of an unrelated illness at the age of fourteen after a long and happy life. But that's not what happened. For every case that has a happy ending, there's one where it doesn't work out. Five months after her surgery, in early December, a grape-sized blister appeared at Pooch's shoulder, exactly at the point where her leg had been amputated. I hardly needed to explain to Geraldine what would have to be done if we were to take treatment further for Pooch: x-rays, ultrasound, biopsies and then an attempt at curative surgery. I agreed with Geraldine's decision not to proceed with this; the chance of a long-term cure was so slim. Instead, I prescribed maximal pain relief, and sent Pooch off to enjoy her last Christmas with her family. In January, just before her eighth birthday, we let her go.

We may have won the first battle by amputating her leg, but that malignant tumour – OK, let's call this one cancer – had won the war.

Questions and answers on tumours

Pets are now living longer lives, thanks to improved nutrition and the advances in veterinary medical care. One down side of this increased longevity is that diseases of advanced age, including cancer, are seen more commonly. Veterinary oncology is a rapidly progressing field, and treatments once confined to human use are now often used in pets. I'm frequently asked questions about pets with tumours: here's a selection.

Last year, my ten-year-old springer spaniel Fern had surgery to remove a gum growth at the front of her mouth. It has come back and is now protruding out of her mouth. Should we get it removed again? Will it keep recurring?

JG, Leicestershire

If any growth is bothering a pet (and this sounds like it is) then removal should be discussed with your vet. This time, request full analysis of the tissue in the laboratory (histopathology) so that your vet knows more about the precise nature of the growth. They'll then be able to make a clearer prediction of whether or not it will recur.

My terrier bitch Tilly (aged ten) adores a neighbour's cross Staffie/boxer Bruno (aged around twelve) who has an inoperable tumour. She has known him since she was a puppy; they have had lots of fun together. What will be the best way to help her deal with his death? I know she will miss him terribly. She cannot walk past his house without putting her nose through the cat flap to greet him.

SR by email

Without wishing to over-humanise Tilly, you should aim to develop a support system for her to help her when Bruno dies. Start now to develop new hobbies and friendships for her. Take her to a doggy day-care centre or even just to your local park so that she can meet other dogs and find additional friends. Take her on outings to new areas, and play novel, interesting games with her. Teach her that there are plenty of fun things in life other than Bruno, so that she'll be less dependent on him. When it happens, you should handle Bruno's death with sensitivity: allow her to see his body shortly after he has passed away. She won't react with obvious grief but anecdotal evidence suggests that dogs may be more accepting of the loss of a companion if they have been allowed to view a lifeless body.

Our fourteen-year-old cat, Jerry, has mouth cancer but we don't want to put him through surgery and radiotherapy to treat him. How will we know when the time is right for us to have him put to sleep? We don't want him to suffer, but neither do we want to deprive him of spending a single extra day with us.

PB & JY, London

This is a dilemma that many pet owners face: how to decide when the time is right. Nobody can tell you the 'right answer' – you and your family know Jerry better than anyone else, so you are the most qualified people to judge his quality of life. Try to force yourself to be objective. Write down a list of everything that Jerry used to enjoy doing in his prime. Then tick everything that he still enjoys doing. If there is a minimal list of ticks, perhaps he is at the stage where there is just not much enjoyment left. Sadly, few pets die peacefully in their sleep at home. The big worry is that they may feel pain but be unable to tell us: intravenous pain infusions on demand, as for human cancer sufferers, are not possible. It often helps to discuss the issues in detail with your vet, or you may wish to use the free-of-charge Blue Cross Pet Bereavement Support Service.

I have just bought three young male rats having just
lost my last two females at around two years of age
with tumours. Are male rats less likely to develop
tumours? I had gone on to a dairy-free diet since
having cancer last year; would a dairy free diet help
the rats remain cancer free? I would be interested to
hear your comments.

PB by email

Unfortunately, cancer is very common in both male and
female rats. As far as I know, the only way to reduce the
incidence is spaying or castration, which definitely helps to
prevent mammary cancer. The lifespan of unneutered rats
is normally only about two years, whereas when they are
spayed or castrated, it is around three years. If you search on
Google for 'cancer in rats' you will find a long list of dietary
ingredients that have been accused of causing cancer in both
male and female rats, but these involve high doses that are
not found in normal rat diets. Rats have often been used in
medical research as models for cancer in humans, which is
why there is so much information available. I would suggest
that you get your male rats castrated, and feed them any
good-quality balanced commercial diet designed for rats.

12

The parrot who refused to talk

One of the biggest challenges of my job as a vet is that my patients can't talk to me. Every day I encounter an animal with a vague disorder that is impossible to define precisely. I would love to be able to ask 'Where is it sore?' or 'What are you feeling?' My job might be far easier in some ways, although there's a possibility that communication from my patients might not always be helpful. The silence of animals makes the job of a vet purer in a sense: there's no distraction from false information being given.

There is one group of patients in my clinic that do talk: parrots, and other similar types of bird. I don't specialise in this area, and I will usually refer complicated cases to a vet who has a particular interest in avian health and disease. But there are some old regulars that I have seen for years, and I will continue to see them as a first care giver, even if I need to send them on to the specialist at some point.

Clint, a twenty-five-year old African grey parrot, is a good example. I got to know his owner, Dan, through his dog originally: he had a lovely Doberman who had died of heart disease at the age of only nine. Dan was so devastated at the loss of his dog that he vowed never to get another. And then he chose an African grey parrot as his next pet partly because he knew that the bird's life expectancy was up to sixty years.

Clint was a hand-reared parrot, bred in captivity. African greys are highly intelligent birds, and perhaps their most remarkable attribute as a pet is the fact that they can mimic human speech. Clint started to talk soon after arriving in Dan's house, and he soon had a rich vocabulary, with a range of words, phrases and idioms, in a variety of accents. Dan was convinced that Clint knew what words meant, and to listen to him, it certainly seemed that way.

So when Dan took out the car keys, Clint would shout, 'Where are you going?' then he'd whistle the tune of 'Don't Leave Me This Way'. When Dan came back, Clint would say, 'I know where you've been, you naughty boy'. In the evenings, Clint would say, 'What's on TV?' or 'Have you got my dinner ready yet' or 'Is it nearly time for bed?' Of course, sceptics would say that Dan was accidentally teaching Clint to say these phrases by giving him specific clues and then rewarding him with praise and attention when he said the right words. But to anyone witnessing Clint talking, it was difficult not to believe that the bird knew exactly what was going on around him.

Clint was unusually close to Dan: he even slept on his bed. This started when the bird was young: he was restless and agitated when left in his cage, and Dan discovered that he settled quickly if allowed out to fly around the bedroom. When Dan switched off the light to go to sleep, Clint fluttered down to his bed, settling down on the top of the duvet, and tucking his head under his wing to sleep.

Clint didn't always have to talk to let Dan know what he wanted. One of his party pieces happened regularly in the middle of the night. Clint would wake Dan up by using his beak to gently tweak the end of his nose. Once Dan was awake, Clint fluttered his wings in front of him, and Dan knew exactly what had to be done. He allowed Clint to perch on his hand while he turned on the light, and went to the bathroom. He then extended one finger, holding it above the open toilet. Clint balanced on the finger, and aimed his droppings straight down the pan. Many parents would wish that their children could aim as well and be as neat and tidy about their toileting as this smart bird. Dan could never recall how this bizarre but useful behaviour started; it was just something that Clint had learned to do.

The first fifteen years of life together for Clint and Dan went smoothly: Dan had read up all about parrot husbandry, so he had the bird on a top-quality diet, and he paid attention to his psychological needs, spending time training him to do small tricks, as well as playing with toys together. Clint was one of the highlights of Dan's life. He used to come in every year for an annual health check, when I'd take bloods to review his routine biochemistry and haematology. The blood sampling was slightly surreal. When I took out the syringe and needle, Clint said 'Uh-oh', moving back to hide inside his owner's jacket. I took the blood sample from the inside of one of his legs, and Clint gave me a running commentary as I did this. 'Stop Stop Stop Stop,' he shouted as I inserted the needle, and then 'Owwww' in a loud shriek as the blood flowed. It was unnerving, but I knew that the bird didn't really mind, as he always allowed me to do the procedure without struggling. Many birds need to be sedated for blood sampling because they're so agitated about the procedure.

Clint's blood results were always normal, which Dan found reassuring: he had the bird's nutrition and health care fine tuned so that it was as good as it could be.

Clint's crisis started when something simple yet traumatic happened. Dan got a girlfriend. Jessica was a glamorous blonde woman in her thirties who met Dan through his hobby of playing bridge. She started to come round to play cards with Dan, and they were soon spending more and more time together. Dan had been worried about how Clint would take this new social aspect to his life. He had expected shrieks of abuse, or fluttering sky dives in an attempt to fluster Jessica. To his surprise, Clint reacted in a far more worrying way. He went completely quiet. Whenever Jessica arrived, Clint would return to his cage, turn his back to the room, and go silent. Dan tried to get him to talk or sing or interact, but Clint completely refused to engage. It was only when Jessica left the building that Clint would liven up again, starting off with a loud wolf whistle before chattering inanities.

Dan persuaded Jessica, who was nervous about birds, to try to engage with Clint, equipping her with treats to offer him, and getting her to sit quietly beside his cage to try to placate him. Clint, however, completely refused to interact.

In time, Dan and Jessica decided it was time for Jessica to move in, and at this stage, Dan was even more worried about how the bird would react. He hoped that Clint would simply get used to the situation, returning to his normal cheerful self, but in fact the reverse happened. Clint withdrew completely, sitting in his cage all day, refusing to talk, even when Jessica wasn't there. It was as if he was depressed. He even started to pick at his food instead of eating hungrily as normal, and he began to lose weight. Dan brought him to me to see if something could be done.

I started by repeating the routine blood tests. For the first time ever, Clint was silent as I collected my sample. I wouldn't have been at all surprised if the bloods had come back showing that he had some sort of virus. He really wasn't himself at all. In fact, the bloods were normal, as they had always been. Yet it was distressing to see Clint the way he was: he was clearly not a happy bird.

I discussed his case online on a parrot discussion board for vets. Some vets specialise in bird behaviour and their advice to me was simple: this bird is depressed and he needs to be treated for this disorder.

How do you treat a depressed bird? The starting point was not dissimilar to advice for a human: anti-depressant medication and one-to-one talking therapy.

I started Clint on a low dose of Valium (diazepam), given as fragments of tablet hidden in a chunk of banana. I also prescribed 'talking therapy', which seemed strange for a bird that was refusing to talk. In practice, this meant that Dan had to spend half an hour, twice daily, specifically engaging with Clint. He bought some new toys, and read up about some new tricks to teach Clint.

For the first week of the treatment regime, both Dan and I felt a little foolish. Were we out of our minds, treating a parrot like a depressed human? Then to the surprise of both of us, Clint began to improve. It started with an increased appetite: he began to nudge Dan with his beak, looking for more when he'd scoffed all the grapes he'd been given. And from then on, he began to talk more, using some of the same language that he'd used in the past. The chatting started during the one-to-one sessions with Dan, but Clint soon began to talk randomly, throughout the day. He was still reticent about Jessica, flying back to his cage when she came into the room, and grumbling quietly, almost under his breath, rather than talking loudly. But on the specialist's advice, Jessica started to take part in the daily training sessions, and it was as if Clint gradually learned to like her. Within a couple of months of his treatment regime starting, Clint was fully back to his old self, and I was able to reduce, then stop, his Valium medication.

If anyone had told me that I would one day be prescribing talking therapy for one of my patients, I'd have told them they were mad. Instead, my conclusion, after witnessing the entire Clint episode, is broader than this: the entire world is mad. Parrots and people are far more similar than any of us would like to believe.

Questions and answers on pet birds

I'm not a specialist avian vet, but I enjoy the variety that birds bring to my daily workload when they are brought to see me. I've also had many questions from readers about their pet birds: here are a few of the unusual ones.

> Is it safe to let my two-year-old cockatoo, Amelia, fly outdoors. I often let her out of her cage to fly around indoors and she loves it, circling around rooms and swooping through doorways. She always comes back to my shoulder when I call her. Would it be too risky to let her out for full open-sky flights?
>
> *FM, Cornwall*

Flight is a wonderful gift that all birds should be allowed to enjoy. Too many cage birds spend their entire lives in a confined space, never stretching their wings and flying. Of course there are risks outside: you should do a formal assessment of the area around your house, noting hazards like fine overhead cables, other wildlife (any birds of prey around?), or busy roads. If you're happy that it's reasonably safe, start with a short flight when she's hungry; she's more likely to come back for a treat. If it goes well, let her fly for longer the next day, and in time, you'll gather confidence in her reliability. Make sure that she's microchipped so that if she did go missing, she'd be identifiable.

> Can birds count? I let my budgie out of his cage every evening, and he always does five circuits of the room before voluntarily returning to his cage. Is this just chance, or does he think one, two, three, etc. as he flies around?
>
> *JB, Bristol*

There's plenty of evidence that birds have a rudimentary ability to count. Scientists have shown that birds can keep a reckoning of the eggs they lay, and I know from my own experience that my Indian Runner duck refuses to sit on her nest until she's laid a minimum of fifteen eggs. Scientists have also done many studies of pigeons and parrots, using blobs on cards to demonstrate that birds can differentiate between different numbers. I doubt that your budgie counts as he circles the room, but if he never does four or six circuits, he clearly has some way of making that judgement.

> We bought a parrot about a year ago and it has suddenly started to use rude words around the house. I think one of my friends is teaching him swear words, while I am out of the room. Any advice?
>
> *GH, Liverpool*

146

Your aim should be to teach him new 'good' words, while making him forget the rude ones. Parrots learn to say words when they get the reward that they seek, which is usually food and social interaction. Say 'good' words to him, and when he repeats them, give him a treat, together with lots of attention. If he ever says a rude word, immediately look away, or even leave the room. This response must be consistent, and you must react instantly, with no delay. Everyone in the house must do this, and you need to have a serious conversation with your foul-mouthed friend. Parrots are usually quick to abandon words that do not have a positive consequence for them.

> I have a kākāriki, which as you'll know is a type of
> New Zealand parakeet. He can be noisy – he makes a
> chattering noise that sounds like a laugh. He seems to
> make this noise more often at times when he could
> actually be laughing at me (e.g. when I stub my toe,
> or drop something accidentally). Is this just my
> imagination or is he teasing me?
>
> JH, Kent

Kakarikis are social birds, and their babbling, chatty vocalisations are part of their charm. Like other parakeets, they react to hearing and seeing humans around them by imitating us. It's a type of interactive activity that they enjoy. When you have these small accidents, you're probably making noises, even without realising it ('Ouch' or 'Darn it' or whatever). The kākāriki is just communicating with you by mimicking your sounds in his own way. Enjoy his interest in you and even try chattering back to him. It'll distract you from your minor misfortunes.

13

The puppy who kept crying

Animals may not be able to talk (apart from parrots) but most pets can vocalise, and this is an important part of how they communicate with owners and vets. The dictionary definition of 'vocalise' is 'to utter something with the voice'. Animals cannot produce words, but they can produce a wide range of sounds, and they use these sounds to express themselves, just as we humans use words.

The story of Ginger illustrates how animals can use sounds to communicate. Ginger was a three-month-old Cavalier King Charles spaniel puppy, almost the definition of cuteness, with a small spherical head, droopy ears, large circular eyes surrounded by a halo of light brown, and a pure white face with a black snubbed nose. Her mouth seemed to be smiling, with the tip of her pink tongue always slightly protruding. She was a healthy, contented puppy, playing enthusiastically, and eating hungrily.

Over a twelve-hour period, everything changed. She became dull and quiet, no longer wanting to play, and she lost all interest in food. When her owner, Finn, reached out his hand to pet her head and reassure her, she backed away, and yelped. She then sat down, looked at him, and whined, letting out a high-pitched keen. He tried to pick her up and comfort her, but she ran to the far corner of the room, and the closer he went to her, the louder she whined.

Finn brought Ginger to see me at once and it was obvious that she had a serious problem. She vocalised continually: with every breath, she whined. Her head seemed to be the epicentre of her discomfort: when anyone put their hand near her face, she started to squeal, but it was difficult to pinpoint the exact source of this pain. She squealed when I examined her, as I tried to find something that could be causing this distress. Was there something stuck inside her mouth? Had she been injured in some way? It was pointless: she wouldn't let me open her mouth at all. I had to work out quickly how I could relieve her obvious discomfort.

I gave her an injection of pain relief and a mild sedative, and checked her into our hospital. After my morning appointments were finished, I examined her again, but even with the drugs numbing her senses, she continued to whine and she still refused to open her mouth.

I moved on to the next stage, giving her a general anaesthetic. This caused her body to relax completely, but to my surprise, even then I was unable to open her mouth more than one inch wide. It was almost as if her mouth had been glued shut. How could this happen? Could she have suffered some unexpected injury, like a broken or dislocated jaw?

I took x-ray pictures of her skull to look beneath the surface, and I was soon viewing the internal structure of the bones and joints of her skull. Everything appeared completely normal.

I knew that there were a few different possible causes of Ginger's severe pain, but initially there was no easy way of finding out precisely what was going on. As vets often do, I decided to treat the signs she was showing, hoping that with time, the problem would naturally begin to resolve. Perhaps it was a bizarre muscle cramp, or perhaps she had badly strained her jaw muscles by chewing something too hard. In either case, she should start to improve after a day or two. I sent her home with strong pain relief, and instructions to offer her tasty, moist, soft food that she would find easy to eat without chewing. The pain-relieving drugs seemed to give her immediate comfort, and by the time she went home, she'd stopped whining. She still didn't want to be touched, but at least the severe distress had begun to settle down.

Ginger came back in to see me two days later. She had developed the first of many complications in her illness.

Her mouth seemed more comfortable, she had stopped vocalising, and she was able to eat again. But she had developed a severe gastrointestinal upset. There are many possible reasons for this type of issue: it's common for puppies to have transient bouts of vomiting and diarrhoea, and often simple treatment is all that's needed. This usually means a short fast, followed by a bland diet for twenty-four hours. In Ginger's case, it also meant that she had to stop all medication, in case this was in some way irritating her stomach and intestines. Of course, the removal of pain-relieving drugs then meant that poor Ginger started to yelp in pain again. For a few days, her medications had to be juggled, trying to reach the right balance of giving her effective control of discomfort without aggravating her digestive upset.

Meanwhile, I was doing some background research about what could be causing her problem. I had sent blood samples to the laboratory for analysis, screening her metabolism for any abnormalities of biochemistry or blood cell counts. As with the x-rays, everything was normal.

I knew that the ideal answer was a specialised test called electromyography (EMG), commonly used in human medicine. Electrical recording apparatus is connected to the patient with probes, to assess the function of different muscle groups. They are rarely used in the veterinary world, and I'd need to refer Ginger to a specialist centre in the UK for this to be carried out. This was on the list of possible next steps, but as I continued to research what else could be done for Ginger, I came across an interesting snippet of information.

A specialised veterinary neuromuscular centre in San Diego had just published a report about eleven Cavalier King Charles spaniel puppies that had developed severe jaw pain, just like Ginger. Full investigations – including electrical tests and even muscle biopsies – had proven that the puppies were suffering from a condition known as masticatory muscle myositis. This rare condition happens when the body develops an immune reaction to its own muscle fibres. The muscle fibres around the jaws are 'rejected', in the same way that a new kidney can be rejected after a kidney transplant. As a result, the muscles become swollen and painful. Once the condition is diagnosed, it can be treated effectively by giving drugs to suppress the immune system.

I sent an email to the San Diego laboratory at once, explaining Ginger's background. They replied within hours, and their response was encouraging. Since the paper had been submitted, they had continued to see small numbers of Cavalier puppies with this problem, and they had developed a special antibody test that could be used to confirm the diagnosis without the need for complicated work ups or muscle biopsies. If I could send them a small blood sample from Ginger, they would be able to confirm the diagnosis. I had already collected blood from Ginger, so I packed it up immediately and sent it off by courier to California. We wouldn't have a result for a few days, but at least we had a hopeful lead on making a definitive diagnosis of the cause of her problem.

At this stage, Ginger was muddling along. Her digestive system had settled down enough for her to take a full dose of pain relief again, and her signs of discomfort had eased. She had stopped yelping, and she was able to eat soft food, albeit slowly. I felt that she was well enough to continue without any other action until we had the results from California.

At this stage, Ginger had another setback. She managed to aggravate a cat in the garden. Nobody saw what happened, but the annoyed cat swiped her across the head, causing a nasty deep scratch to her right eye. Ginger had to be rushed to a specialist eye surgeon for emergency surgery to repair her lacerated cornea. She recovered well, but at this stage she seemed to be the most unfortunate puppy in the world, with a new health challenge every week.

It took two weeks for the results to arrive from California, and the email from the laboratory carried the news that Ginger was definitely suffering from masticatory muscle myositis. With a definitive diagnosis, I was able to change her treatment to a specific, well-established regime that I knew would help her. I started her on a high level of immunosuppressive drugs to stop her body from rejecting her own jaw muscles. She responded well: the yelping stopped completely, and she began to behave like a normal puppy.

Ginger still had problems: her head muscles were scarred after the attack from her own immune system. The normal elastic flexibility of the muscles had stiffened up, and she remained unable to open and close her mouth like a normal puppy. Her tongue lolled out of her mouth in a strange way, and she couldn't open her mouth as widely as a normal pup. When I examined her, it no longer hurt her to have her mouth opened, but the scar tissue meant that her jaws could only separate by a couple of inches, rather than the full yawn-like gaping of a normal animal. This problem is technically known as trismus, and in theory, I could have attempted treatment by forcing her jaw to open wider under anaesthesia, tearing the scar tissue. To me, this seemed a brutal form of therapy, and it wasn't needed. She could open her mouth enough to live a normal life, and she was pain-free. She wasn't perfect, but she was happy.

As she matured, Ginger ended up being smaller than her litter mates, but her diminutive size, combined with her long-term illnesses, seemed to endear her even more to the humans around her. She was genetically weak and physically afflicted, but her bright, strong personality allowed her to rise above her problems.

There was one odd aspect to her story. Her loud, shrill vocalising was the feature of her illness that made people realise that she was unwell. But once she'd been treated, she never vocalised again. She didn't bark, whine, cry or whimper: once she'd been cured, she became a completely silent dog.

Questions and answers on pet vocalisations

Pets are experts in non-verbal communication, but there are times when they resort to the use of their voice boxes in their efforts to impart messages to the humans around them. Here's a selection of queries about vocalising pets that I've dealt with over the years.

We have adopted a rescue petit basset griffon Vendéen who came to us in very poor condition. He is now a handsome specimen, with most of his problems sorted except for his howling. This generally starts at around 4 a.m. when he will howl for one to two minutes. He then howls intermittently till 8 a.m., and he's quiet for the rest of the day. We are increasingly desperate for a full night's sleep. Can you please advise us?

LM, Lancaster

Some dogs are prone to howling, either as a call for attention or as an announcement that something is happening. Your dog seems to be howling for both of these reasons. You should do all that you can to make his environment as comforting as possible, including putting on a radio, with classical music playing, in the background, and plugging in an Adaptil diffuser to release calming pheromones around his bed. You should talk to your vet about giving him a mild sedative last thing at night, so that he has a deeper, longer-lasting sleep. Remember that any kind of accidental reinforcement on your part may maintain this behaviour. Talking to him, touching him, letting him out, or giving him any other positive experience will encourage him to keep howling, even if you just do it occasionally.

I thought that cats only purred when they were contented, but Roly, my neutered ginger tom purrs almost continually, even when he's under stress. The latest example was at the vet: Roly was anxious, trying to jump off the table, but he continued to purr so loudly that the vet couldn't hear his heart with the stethoscope. Why do cats purr and are there any tricks for stopping him from purring (e.g. for his next heart check-up)?

AB, Northants

A cat's purr is not just about contentment. Cat experts say that the purr happens when 'positive social interaction is taking place or when it's desired'. I've also heard it described as happening when a cat has a friend, or needs a friend. Cats purr in all sorts of situations. The classical example may be a contented cat curled up on your lap, but I've seen cats purring even when they're in pain, after being injured. I have my own trick for stopping cats purring when trying to listen to their heart and lungs: if a tap in the sink is turned on, most cats stop purring for a few minutes while looking at, and listening to, the running water.

> Our five-year-old Siamese cat roars at us continuously. There are times when we have to put him out of the room so that we can have a normal conversation. What can we do to shut him up?
>
> *YP by email*

Siamese cats often have loud voices that seem to reach the precise pitch designed to be most annoying to humans. I'd suggest that you get him checked by your vet to make sure that he doesn't have any underlying disease (e.g. high blood pressure can cause cats to scream like banshees). Once you know he's healthy, try to enrich his environment as much as possible. Give him boxes or bags to explore, toys that release food gradually, and if he enjoys catnip, indulge him with it. Try different toys to entertain him; the idea is to use up his energy with physical activity rather than miaowing. A Feliway pheromone diffuser will help him feel more relaxed, and as a final resort, you may wish to talk to your vet about calming medication for a period while you teach him quieter, more social habits.

When I listen to certain types of music (particularly soprano singing), my current dog (a five-year-old German shepherd bitch) starts howling loudly. She continues to do so until I turn off or change the music. None of my previous dogs has behaved in this way. I would like to know why she howls and if she's distressed by the music pitch.

FH by email

Howling is a natural communication method for dogs; the sound carries further than barks or growls. It's how dogs talk to each other over longer distances, to pass on messages to each other, or to summon the pack together. No one knows why some dogs howl more than others. It just seems to be a peculiarity of some individuals. Howling doesn't mean that a dog is upset in any way, although it's true that dogs do sometimes howl when distressed (e.g. some dogs with separation anxiety howl when left on their own). I suspect that if your dog strongly disliked the music, she'd try to leave the room. It's more likely that the soprano is hitting notes that remind your dog of another dog howling, and she's joining in joyfully. It's a bit like a human singing along to a favourite song on the radio and it's nothing to worry about at all.

14

The cat who drank
too much

Chico was a large striking-looking black cat with yellow eyes: he had a panther-like quality about him. His owner Rhona knew him well: when you live with a cat, you learn about their daily activities, moods, routines and likes and dislikes. Cats, like humans, tend to be predictable creatures.

She brought him to see me because over a period of a few weeks she had noticed that something was not quite right. She could not put her finger on exactly what was wrong, but she knew he was not himself. An owner's intuition is one of the most sensitive barometers of a pet's health. When a pet is unwell, the first sign of illness is often subtle, but to pet owners it's often obvious that their pet is 'not their normal self'. Taking your pet to the vet promptly is often worth doing, as early diagnosis and treatment of some illnesses makes the difference between life and death.

When Chico was lifted onto my consulting table, my first impression was that he seemed to be a bright, cheerful, friendly cat. He pushed his head against my hand, purring loudly. Before examining him closely, I spent some time petting him, watching him from a distance, and I asked Rhona some questions.

Her main worry was simply that Chico was behaving differently to normal. Chico had been less active and energetic, and was spending more time sleeping. He was normally a keen hunter, bringing mice and birds back several times a week, but he hadn't caught anything for the previous month. He seemed quieter and less engaging than normal. She also thought that he had lost weight, despite the fact that he seemed as hungry as ever, and she was feeding him as much food as usual. I put him on our electronic scales, and they confirmed that he had lost 10 per cent of his body weight since his last visit. He was still a big cat, but he had gone down from 6.6kg to 6kg. This was like a ten-stone person going down to nine stone: not something to ignore.

Rhona also felt that Chico seemed to be 'rounder' than before: his normal lean, trim profile seemed to have gone soft around the middle, with a pot belly. I wasn't convinced this was a big issue: just like older humans, many older cats lose their abdominal muscle tone. And when I carefully examined his abdomen, pressing from one side to the other, everything felt normal: there were no swellings, gatherings of fluid or painful areas.

I asked Rhona some specific questions about other aspects of Chico's life. In most tangible ways, he seemed very normal. No digestive upsets, no coughing, no itchiness, no lameness.

She wasn't sure how to answer one important question: how much water did he drink? Vets know how much cats are supposed to drink: there's a formula of millilitres per kilogram. While it's common for a cat to drink less than this, if they drink more, there's a problem. This concept is sometimes more theoretical than useful in practice. Like many cats, Chico was private about his drinking habits. He spent most of his days in the garden where he was likely to drink from puddles and ponds. His indoor bowl was just for occasional top-ups. When I pressed Rhona, she thought she'd seen Chico at his water bowl more often recently, and she had topped it up twice in the previous week, whereas she normally just topped it up once.

I moved on to examine Chico. He seemed remarkably normal: I could find nothing amiss other than his belly being a little more rotund than it used to be.

Cases like Chico often require science to be summoned to investigate the inner workings of the body. I decided to take a blood sample to do a broad analysis of his blood biochemistry. While we were waiting for the results, I gave him a broad spectrum worm tablets: as a hunter, Chico would be likely to pick up tapeworms from the small prey that he caught, and these could cause the weight loss and pot belly.

I was relieved, yet still puzzled, when Chico's blood results were ready: they were almost completely normal. There was one abnormality, but it was more of a question mark than a bullseye. Chico's blood glucose was 30 per cent higher than normal. Just as in humans, a high blood glucose can indicate diabetes, when the pancreas stops producing the hormone insulin which keeps the blood glucose within set limits. The challenge in making this diagnosis in cats is that they are prone to having high blood glucose levels when stressed, and a visit to the vet clinic can be one of the best ways to stress a cat. So was Chico's high blood glucose a sign of illness or of a cat feeling edgy?

Diabetes used to be rare in cats, but it's seen more commonly now that cats are fed on richer diets leading to expanding waistlines. The signs of diabetes certainly fitted Chico's story: weight loss despite increased appetite, lethargy and increased thirst are all classic findings.

I asked Rhona to leave Chico with us for a day. I settled him into our cat-only hospital ward, with its special large cages infused with calming cat pheromones and comfy cushions. I left him in peace for the day, calling in to chat to him every couple of hours. During our conversation, I quietly slipped the tiniest, sharpest needle into one of the pads of his back feet. I just needed a drop of blood to measure his blood glucose on each visit, and he barely noticed this happening. The series of test results gave me a graph of Chico's blood glucose measurements over a twelve-hour period: a so-called glucose curve. If his high glucose was a stress reaction, I'd see jerky peaks during his times of anxiety. As it was, his glucose stayed steadily and consistently well above normal. There was no doubt about the diagnosis: Chico was diabetic.

The standard form of treatment of diabetes in cats is twice daily injections of insulin for the rest of the pet's life. Rhona, like most people, had no experience of giving injections, never mind holding down an independent-minded cat to do so. She didn't believe it would be possible and pleaded with me: surely there must be some other way?

A special high-protein, low-carbohydrate diet can help some cats with diabetes, and in a few cases, this can be enough to bring the blood glucose right back to normal. We decided on a compromise: we would try Chico on the special diet for a week, and Rhona would use the week to practise her injection skills on an orange. She'd learn the knack of holding the syringe properly, inserting the needle smoothly, and depressing the plunger confidently. Once she was adept on an orange, she'd be less nervous to doing the same to Chico.

The truth is the syringe needles are sharp and fine, and the amount of insulin to be injected into a cat is tiny. The scruff of a cat's neck – the injection site – is a relatively pain-insensitive zone (think about kittens being carried by the scruffs of their necks). Most cats barely notice the injection being given.

The blood tests after a week of special nutrition confirmed that Chico still had elevated blood glucose, and he definitely needed a twice-daily dose of insulin. Rhona, now an orange-injecting expert, was nervous as she gave Chico his first injection under my tutelage. He was busily tucking into his dinner as she gave it, and he didn't even seem to notice. I sent her home, equipped with syringes, insulin bottles, and sharps containers to store the used needles.

I texted Rhona the following morning to find out how the first injection on her own had gone. Her reply summarised things neatly: 'Chico enjoyed his breakfast, the job is done and I'm now enjoying my own breakfast.'

Chico returned to 'his old self' within a few days. His energy levels returned, he stopped sleeping as much, and he began to leave mice and birds at the back door again. Rhona had never enjoyed these 'gifts', but for the first time, she was quietly pleased to see them. Her panther cat had returned.

Questions and answers on pet drinking habits

The level of a pet's water consumption is something that most owners aren't aware of: it's only when they start to drink a lot that people are prompted to pay attention. It's a common and important clue to underlying illnesses. Here are some of the questions that people have sent me relating to their pet's drinking habits.

We have an eleven-year-old West Highland white terrier who has developed diabetes. She was diagnosed about six months ago. She seems fit and well in herself and sees the vet regularly for blood tests; however, she still drinks a lot and floods the kitchen floor every night with urine. If the insulin is doing its job, shouldn't she have a normal thirst and be able to control her bladder? Is this just becoming a habit, or should I change my vet?

ST by email

It isn't normal for a well-controlled diabetic dog to continue to have this problem. Some diabetics can have routine blood tests that appear normal, yet when more detailed investigations are done (such as a twenty-four-hour 'blood glucose curve', with samples collected every two hours), it can become apparent that further fine-tuning of insulin dosage is needed. In other cases, analysis of a urine sample is needed, because kidney infection is a common complication in diabetics, and this can cause the same signs. Finally, it's possible that she has another underlying issue, such as liver disease. You don't need to change vets, but you do need to go back to your own vet and explain what's happening.

> A male cat that visits our garden is very thin, balding and drinks a lot of water. I have been to see his owners several times and have asked them to take him to the vets but they don't seem interested. What can I do?
>
> AD, Guernsey

The cat needs to visit the vet so that the problem can be identified and treated. It could be kidney or liver disease, diabetes, thyroid disease or many other possibilities. If you want to help the cat, you need to take the initiative, asking the owner if you can take him to the vet on their behalf, even offering to pay the costs. He may need a special diet and daily medication, so be aware that this could be a big commitment for you, but if you want to help him, I can't see another way.

> We are taking our dog to France this summer on holiday. When we're on the continent, we always drink bottled water. Should we give this to our dog too, or will it be OK to give him water from the tap?
>
> SF, Norwich

Most dogs have robust constitutions, and they're much more able than humans to cope with minor issues of drinking water quality. Dogs are happy to drink water from muddy ditches and stagnant ponds, and they rarely suffer serious adverse consequences. Tap water in Europe won't cause your dog any harm. The one problem that I can envisage is that it may have a different taste to the water than he's used to, and for this reason he may not like it. It's important that he keeps up his drinking so that he doesn't get dehydrated on his travels. For this reason only, you may wish to offer him some of your bottled water. If he prefers this to the local tap water, then it makes sense to let him drink it.

I have been told that I should not feed my Chinese hamster anything remotely sweet – even such as peas and corn – as this species is exceptionally prone to diabetes. He enjoys eating little pieces of apple, carrot or strawberries – but is it OK to feed him these? And what about the hamster yoghurt drops or any other sweeter treats?

RL, South Yorkshire

A high proportion of Chinese hamsters are born with a genetic predisposition to developing diabetes; the species has been studied extensively in the laboratory as a model for human diabetes. If your hamster has this genetic make-up, then you can delay or prevent the onset of diabetes by careful attention to his diet. The aim is to feed a high-protein, low-sugar, low-fat diet, so sweet fruit and commercial hamster treats should not be given. For a full list of suitable foods, visit my blog at www.petethevet.com. Signs of diabetes in hamsters include weight loss, cataracts and an increased thirst, so if these develop, you should discuss treatment possibilities with your vet.

15

The dog who kept the wheels turning

Vets have a secret weapon, exclusive to our profession. It's the ultimate in pain relief, but it can be used only in the most hopeless circumstances. When used, it takes away all pain, permanently. It's highly effective, but there is a serious and incurable side effect: it also causes death.

I am talking about euthanasia, sometimes referred to as the most extreme form of palliative care. Vets are fortunate to be able to offer relief in this way: when animals are suffering from advanced, painful cancer, when elderly animals are in the final stages of old-age degeneration and indignity, and when the future for a pet will involve only discomfort and inevitable distress.

Of course, euthanasia can easily be misused: nearly all vets are sometimes asked to euthanase healthy animals, and this can present ethical challenges. A pet's owner is allowed to make this decision: ending a life prematurely may seem unfair, but the law doesn't regard it as cruel, as long as the animal doesn't suffer pain or suffering during the process. Most vets have their own ethical stance on this, and few will euthanase a pet without clear justification. Examples of when euthanasia is requested for healthy animals include dogs with serious, untreatable and dangerous aggression, animals with incontinence so severe that they cannot live hygienically in a human home, and pets with severe psychiatric disease causing behaviour that's incompatible with sharing their lives with humans.

While some euthanasia decisions are clear-cut, there are many situations where a call could be made either way. Sally the Labrador was one such case.

Sally had the best attributes of her breed: she was smart, sociable and good-natured, one of those animals that everyone loved. People would ask Suzanne if they could play with her, or take selfies with her. Sally was always friendly to everyone, enjoying meeting new people and delighting in the company of other dogs.

It was a calm, sunny autumn day when the crisis of Sally's life happened, on her daily walk with Suzanne. She habitually walked off the lead, calmly and predictably staying by Suzanne's side. On this occasion, Sally had a momentary but life-changing blip in her routine: she unexpectedly dashed out into the road. Suzanne never found out what made her do this, but the consequence of this fleeting unpredictability was devastating.

She was hit full on her side by a passing car, thrown into the air and flung onto the verge. At first, as Sally lay not moving, Suzanne thought that she'd been killed outright – the force had been so severe that Suzanne couldn't imagine any animal could survive.

Then Sally started to keen, a high-pitched series of loud squeals. Suzanne knew at once that she was alive, in serious pain and badly injured. She rushed over to her, talking to her and reassuring her while trying to work out what she could do to help her.

The driver of the car was understandably upset, even though there was no way that he could have avoided hitting her. With Suzanne's quiet calming voice in her ear, Sally soon stopped crying, and the man helped to lift her slowly and carefully on to a large blanket. Using this as a makeshift stretcher, they lifted her into the back of his car and headed for our clinic.

Vet clinics are set up to be ready to deal with acute emergencies. I was in the middle of a busy morning session of routine appointments when a nurse interrupted me. 'Pete: there's badly injured dog here. We need you now.' Sally had been carried in to our emergency room. She was still quietly whimpering, so my first action was to give her potent opiate pain relief intravenously. As the drug dulled her pain, her body visibly relaxed.

X-rays would be taken later, but I could tell from a simple physical examination that Sally's back had been broken: there was a 'step' defect on her spine, which meant there could be no other diagnosis. Her hind legs were paralysed, and there was no prospect of her ever walking again. Sally was set up on intravenous fluids for shock, and placed in a warm, soft-bedded kennel. Once she'd been stabilised, I left Suzanne with her while I cleared my routine appointments. I then returned to have that difficult conversation.

I spelled out the facts to Suzanne, telling her the truth: Sally could never have the same life that she'd had. There was a risk that she might die of her internal injuries, and if she survived, she would never walk again. Also, she'd be doubly incontinent, losing voluntary control of urination and defecation. In this situation, most owners feel that their pet's quality of life is likely to be so poor they would choose euthanasia. As I spoke, Sally gazed at Suzanne with sparkling, bright eyes. The pain relief had worked, but she was fully aware of her surroundings. Suzanne told me her decision: 'Sally wants to live. So I want to do everything to make her life as good as it can possibly be.'

Sally stayed in our clinic for the next four days, and Suzanne researched paralysed dogs on the internet. I guided her to websites set up to help people in similar situations.

She soon discovered that life can carry on for many paralysed dogs, as long as an owner is prepared to make the effort and investment needed to help. Meanwhile, we treated Sally with rest, pain relief and gentle physiotherapy to prepare her for a new life at home. There was nothing else we could do; her broken back could not be repaired.

The main challenge was her mobility: while Sally's front legs were fully functional, her back legs were completely paralysed, and would drag behind her if she tried to walk. With wheels to support her hindquarters, she would be able to move around easily. To start with, a friend made an improvised wheelchair from a child's buggy. Sally took to it immediately, tearing around as if she had been born on wheels.

After a year, the wheels started falling off, and Suzanne had to look at different long-term options. She found an American company that makes custom-designed canine wheelchairs. Their website had a Facebook page full of discussions with other owners of paralysed dogs, and reading their stories, Suzanne began to appreciate the potential value of a wheelchair designed by someone who had already supplied wheelchairs to thousands of paralysed dogs. Suzanne sent off Sally's measurements, and soon after, a state-of-the-art wheelchair arrived from America. Sally now has air-filled tyres like those on a mountain bike, and she's able to run around off-road.

As with any paralysed dog, there are practical challenges. The wheelchair harness needs to be monitored carefully to make sure that pressure sores don't develop. Toileting is a complicated and ongoing issue: Suzanne needs to squeeze Sally's abdomen several times a day, to keep her bladder emptied, and Sally doesn't have normal control of her faeces either. But with care and planning, Suzanne is able to manage the situation. Several times a day, she lifts Sally out of her wheelchair, gently pressing her abdomen from beneath, to empty her bladder. And although she has no voluntary control of defecation, her digestive system works in a predictable way, so that in the hour after eating, faeces are produced. Suzanne knows when to look out for this, clean her promptly and efficiently. Suzanne and Sally have learned that a careful, regular routine is needed to keep these bodily functions under control. Some paralysed dogs suffer from issues like urine scalding (when urine spills out of the bladder, burning the skin under the tail) and pressure sores, but thankfully, Sally has been spared these. Suzanne's methodical dedication to her daily care has been the key to success in this area.

Sally is an unusual dog in Ireland, and she draws much attention. Often a crowd forms, with people queuing up to meet Sally and to talk to Suzanne. Everyone wants to know what happened to her, and they're amazed at her ability to rush around on wheels. Nowadays, I only see Sally for her twice-yearly vet check-up and I enjoy her visits immensely. She reminds me, every time, that our daily problems are largely in our own heads rather than caused by the physical circumstances around us. If a dog can have a happy, active life despite the fact that she has a badly broken back, there's a strong message there for us able-bodied humans.

Questions and answers on problems with mobility

It's easy to take the nimble dexterity of pets for granted, but especially with aging animals, issues with mobility are common. Here are some of the queries that readers have raised with me about their pets' impaired ability to move around.

> Our seven-year-old Dalmatian, Diesel, suffers from debilitating arthritis. He has been on Metacam and a glucosamine supplement, as prescribed by our vet. A family member (human!) with arthritis takes a supplement called CherryActive so we have started Diesel on this, with doses modified to his size. He does appear to be more mobile and more cheerful. We have tried to investigate whether CherryActive is safe to give to dogs but cannot find any information.
>
> *CF, Chingford*

CherryActive is a nutritional extract, made from Montmorency cherries, said to be rich in anti-oxidants. The product is available as a capsule and as a liquid concentrate. As it's made from only cherries there should not be any problems with toxicity. Like many similar products, it can be difficult to establish whether or not there is a positive effect on the arthritis in the absence of properly conducted clinical trials.

Make sure that you let your vet know that you're giving this product, in case any issues, positive or negative, arise in the future. Most dogs with arthritis benefit from a patchwork of treatments as well as modern drugs, including weight control, exercise moderation, nutritional supplements, and even novel interventions such as physiotherapy, hydrotherapy and acupuncture.

> My ten-year-old Labrador has arthritis. I've bought a dog ramp as she can't jump into the car anymore (and I can't lift her). However, no amount of encouragement persuades her to use it. I've tried putting it flat on the ground indoors to get her comfortable with it but she just runs and hides! Is it possible to teach an old dog new tricks?
>
> *HS, Norfolk*

Advancing age makes learning slower for both humans and animals, but none of us is ever too old to pick up new skills. You need to consistently give your dog a reward for carrying out any new behaviour that you want her to. A reward is whatever she likes: it may be food treats, a favourite toy or activity, lots of praise from you, or anything else that she enjoys. If you consistently reward her, she'll soon want to do the new behaviour. If she's not used to obeying commands, you may need to train her without the ramp first, just to walk towards you for a treat. When she does this reliably, start to include the ramp, flat on the ground. Repeat the training every day for fifteen minutes, starting to include a slight incline on the ramp. Within a few weeks, you'll have her using it as you wish.

> Our twelve-month-old border collie has had surgery to pin a broken humerus. He won't be allowed an off-the-lead walk for quite some time. Do you have any ideas for games to mentally stimulate him? We have exhausted hide and seek already!
>
> *LC, Surrey*

If a dog is restricted to lead walks you need to be cautious: any kind of play, including hide and seek, is likely to generate loads that are greater than normal walking, placing extra pressure on healing bones. Instead, to tire him out, consider games that involve training. Burning up mental energy can leave him as worn out as if he had gone for an energetic run. As an example, using clicker training, dogs can be taught to learn the names of objects. One border collie (@ChasertheBC on Twitter) has learned the names of over a thousand objects. To learn how to do this, watch this YouTube video: http://youtu.be/9cDzgEa4Ado. To find out more about clicker training, see www.clickertraining.com.

We have a large eight-year-old neutered tom-cat
who has always been nimble, but lately he has been
struggling to jump up onto our bed or sofa. He
scrambles, rather than jumping gracefully. Should we
take him to the vet?

PM, London

There are many possibilities here, from arthritis to spinal
disease to general ill health. It was only when my own five-
year-old cat started stumbling when leaping that I was
prompted to listen to his chest with a stethoscope, and I
found an irregular heart beat. He responded to treatment,
and now jumps normally again. You don't need to commit
yourself to major (and costly) investigations at this stage,
but an initial physical examination by your vet is definitely
a good idea.

16

The big cat who
wasn't a fat cat

Most cats arrive at my vet clinic in cat carrier cages, usually carried in by the owner. When Gabrielle arrived, pulling her large plastic cat carrier in to see me on a wheeled trolley designed for pulling a heavy suitcase around an airport, I knew that I must be dealing with some sort of unusual situation. What was lurking inside the carrier?

I bent down to lift the cat carrier onto the consulting table, almost wrenching my back as I attempted to pick it up with one hand. Even using both hands around the base of the carrier it was a struggle to hoist the load onto the table.

I peered through the door into the carrier, expecting to see two or three cats inside, but to my surprise, there was just one animal looking back at me. He was one of the biggest cats

I have ever seen. I opened the carrier door, and as I coaxed Mugley to come out, Gabrielle explained his background.

Mugley was a stray cat who had wandered into Gabrielle's life some years previously. As many cats do, he had turned up at the back door one day, looking for food and a little attention. He was friendly, so Gabrielle fed him and allowed him into her warm kitchen. He came and went that first day, but when he came back a few days later, he stayed for good. The mystery of his origin remained: did he have a home that he had grown tired of? Cats often decide to move on if a household doesn't suit them. Perhaps a newly arrived dog annoyed him? Could there have been too many other cats in a small space? Or as Gabrielle was later to wonder, could it have been that the daily food ration wasn't to his liking?

Mugley had seemed like a large adult cat when he arrived, and Gabrielle presumed that he was fully grown. It can be difficult to tell the age of cats, even for vets. As the months passed, it became obvious that he had only been an adolescent. Mugley ate twice as much as any other animal in her home, and he continued to grow, soon dwarfing her other normal-sized adult cats. Eventually he stopped growing, but he was now so big that Gabrielle began to worry about him. He didn't seem obese in the traditional, broad-backed, pot-bellied, blubber-coated style. He was just immense, with a build like a modern professional rugby player. Gabrielle began to wonder if Mugley had become overweight. Or was he just 'large framed' and muscular? She decided to bring him to see me for a professional opinion.

Pet obesity is shockingly common across the spectrum of animals kept in modern homes. Dogs, cats, rabbits, hamsters and budgies are all often affected. Surveys have demonstrated that around one third of all pets are too fat, a grotesque statistic in a world where human children still die from hunger-related causes. This pet obesity phenomenon is much more complicated than it may at first seem. Pets do not become fat because owners deliberately overindulge their beloved pets; often there's a basic misunderstanding of the nutritional needs and habits of animals, combined with the emotional challenge of saying 'no' to an animal that enjoys being given treats.

Humans have evolved as hunter/gatherers. We are genetically programmed to catch and collect food, store it, then eat it in small quantities as needed. We instinctively know that it would be foolish to eat every crumb in the cupboard: our large forebrain allows us to plan for tomorrow, ensuring a steady food supply.

Cats and dogs, on the other hand, have descended from predators and/or scavengers. Their ancestors hunted prey, or found the remains of prey that had been killed by others. They had to eat it rapidly, while keeping an eye out for another predator sneaking up to steal their food and perhaps to attack them as well. The most successful plan is to eat quickly then move on promptly. Wild carnivores do not store food around them in the same way as humans. Instead, they store food inside their body as fat. When this is understood, it's easy to see why dogs and cats are prone to developing obesity when living in the food-rich environment of a modern household.

Most pet owners don't understand their pet's attitude to food. They believe that if their pet wants to eat, that must mean that they're hungry, and that it's somehow unfair to deprive a hungry pet of food. Pets are experts at reading human body language, and they soon learn that if they look at their owner in a certain way, perhaps with head tilted to one side, and a sorrowful expression on the face, they will be offered more food. And being genetically geared to eat as much as possible on the spot, they just keep eating.

Just as in humans, pet obesity has many adverse consequences,. First, there's a vicious circle of increasing girth. The fatter a pet becomes, the less they want to exercise, and the less energy they burn up. They become bored, and the most enjoyable part of their life is eating, so they eat more. Fat pets are prone to a range of health issues, from diabetes, to heart disease, to arthritis. They live shorter, less enjoyable lives. And the worst thing is that it is not their fault, nor is it a random occurrence: obesity is a direct consequence of the actions of the human looking after them.

The celebrities of our modern world are perhaps among the leanest, fittest-looking people of all, and there's an obvious reason for that: they have personalised nutritionists and fitness trainers. The good news for pets is that their human owners are in the perfect position to become unpaid diet and exercise coaches. We control exactly what pets eat, and how they exercise. If they are overweight, in theory, we can easily adjust their food intake and level of energy expenditure to fine-tune their body condition.

In practice, it's not so easy. Habitual ways of interacting are difficult to change. There is no easy answer: it's as much about the human psychology of modifying ingrained owner behaviour as it is about the apparently simple task of giving a pet less food and more exercise.

When a pet has become fat, it isn't enough just to start to feed the correct amount of food. Ultra-strict rations are needed in the early stages, using measured amounts of special low-calorie pet food. Owners need to stick rigidly to carefully planned feeding and exercise plans, and the success rate is low. Instead of waiting until a pet has grown grossly obese, it's far easier to identify a trend to obesity earlier on. If a standard, simple, normal diet is introduced at that stage, it's far easier to regain and maintain a healthy body shape.

So the big question is, 'How do you tell if a pet is getting fat?' And when is a pet simply a large-framed animal? This was the question that Gabrielle wanted me to answer about Mugley when she wheeled him in to see me that day.

Vets have been trained to review three main parameters when assessing a pet's body condition.

First, can the bones of the spine be felt if you run your hand along the pet's back? If an animal is too fat, the layer of blubber along the back can make it impossible to feel the normal hard ridges of the spinal vertebrae.

Second, can you feel the ribs if you place your hand on the side of the pet's chest? The ribs should not be so prominent that you can see them easily, but as you run your fingers along your pet's chest, you should be able to feel the washboard-like contour of the bones of the ribs.

Third, look down at the overall shape of your pet from above. Pets should have an hour-glass type shape: widest at the chest, narrow around the midriff, and then wider at the pelvis. Fat pets become like shapeless cushions, wide at the chest, equally wide at the midriff and wide again at the pelvis. You can also assess your pet from the side. Animals should have a vaguely triangular, wedge-shaped outline: wider at the front, and tapering up towards their rear ends. Obese cats are particularly prone to losing this shape, developing a spherical shape from the side, with their bellies drooping down almost to touch the ground.

After eventually extracting Mugley from his carrier, I examined him critically. His body shape was close to ideal. He was lean and well-muscled all over, and he had a long, lithe body shape, with a tucked-up abdomen. I could feel his bones easily, and his silhouette was the right shape from every angle.

Mugley is simply a huge cat. When I put him on the scales, he weighed in at over 9kg. He was heavier than many fat cats, but obesity was not a problem for him. He had a big appetite because he had a large frame to maintain.

I told Gabrielle that she could carry on feeding him in exactly the same way as she had been doing so far. I also suggested that it'd be a good idea to get a bigger cat carrier. A giant cat deserves a giant carrying cage, even if his owner feels as if she needs a personal porter in which to carry him around.

Questions and answers on pet nutrition

Healthy eating is as important to pets as it is to humans, and they have an advantage: they can't go to the fridge to help themselves. Pets' owners are in control, but they're often not sure what to do. Here are some of the questions I've answered about pet nutrition.

Can gerbils get fat? I left my three-year-old gerbil, Jimmy, with a friend when I was away on holiday, and when I returned, he looked larger than before, with a more curvaceous body. Jimmy is a fussy eater, picking out the sunflower seeds from his mix, because he likes them most. I am strict with him, and I make sure that I don't give him too many of them, but I think my friend may have been spoiling him. Do you think this is possible, or worse: do you think my Jimmy might have died and been secretly replaced with a different, larger gerbil?

KW, Winchester

Firstly, pick up the little fellow, and look him in the eye. You will know right away if the gerbil is not your Jimmy. Pet owners like yourself get to know their own pets so well that it is very hard to be deceived. In any case, it is far more likely that Jimmy has just over-indulged himself in your absence. Your friend will have been worried about under-feeding him, and has probably over-compensated by giving him too much. Sunflower seeds are very high in energy, and gerbils are just as prone to obesity as any animal if they are given too many calories. You should put Jimmy back onto his normal diet, and I am sure he will slim back to his normal shape before too long.

> My cat Fox absolutely loves raw chicken eggs and will come running at the sound of a shell being broken. He would eat at least one a day if I let him. I am concerned that one a day is too much. I am thinking of cholesterol. How many a week should I let him have? Can cats be affected by cholesterol in the way that humans are?
>
> *CM, Winchester*

High cholesterol is bad for humans because it is linked to the common problem of atherosclerosis, or hardening of the arteries, which is associated with heart disease. Cats (and other pets) do not suffer from this problem at all, so you do not need to worry about this aspect of egg-eating. However, all pets do need to be fed a balanced diet in moderate quantities. One egg a day is fine for your cat, as long as the rest his diet consists of standard good-quality cat food, and as long as he is not prone to obesity. You should also be aware that raw eggs carry a low risk of salmonella infection, but this is less likely in cats than in humans.

My pet rabbit Winston has become obese. I'm trying to lose weight myself, and I have strict rules about dieting and exercise. Should I make similar plans for Winston? In the past, I've given him treats such as honey sticks and yoghurt-coated nibbles. Can you buy low-calorie rabbit treats, and how can I get him to take more exercise?

MW, Scunthorpe

Even without sugary treats, most pet rabbits consume too many calories. A bowl piled high with concentrated cereal mix provides far more energy than a rabbit can burn up hopping quietly around a small garden. Cut back Winston's daily dry food ration by 50 per cent, and offer him plenty of high-quality hay instead. If you must give treats, try the ones made of plant leaves, like alfafa, that have been rolled together into cigar-like shapes. For exercise, spend time playing with him. Chase him around the garden. Most rabbits love running games, and you'll end up out of breath yourself, which will help your own fitness goals. Finally, monitor his progress: ask your local vet clinic to weigh him on electronic scales every month.

Our five-year-old spayed female Labrador, Elsie, is overweight, and she's always hungry. If we don't give her more food, she sits there gazing at us, pleading with her eyes. When we're having our dinner, she actually salivates. We end up giving in and letting her have more food. How can we get her to lose weight without being cruel to her?

BB by email

There's a difference between 'being hungry' and 'wanting food', and I suspect Elsie falls into the latter category. If she is overweight, then her body does not need extra calories, and as long as there's no food to see or smell, she's unlikely to be genuinely hungry. You need to take a firm line; don't give in to her pleading. Leave her in a different room when you're eating to spare her the tantalising odour of your own food. You need to be objective about a weight-loss programme. Get her weighed every fortnight at your local vet clinic. Weigh out her food ration every day. Reduce the amount you feed her by a small amount every week until she starts to lose weight. Maintain this smaller food portion until she has reached a normal weight. Once she's reached this level, you can start to give her a little more again. If you're still having problems, consider a special prescription weight-reduction diet (such as Hills R/D), which is high in fibre but low in calories. This should give her a better sense of 'fullness' while keeping her calorie intake down to a minimum.

17

The swan who flew with a broken wing

The waiting room in a vet clinic is rarely boring. One Tuesday afternoon, the usual assortment of dogs on leads and cats in carriers at our practice presented a calm and ordinary scene. Then the front door clattered open, and two women staggered in holding a swan between them. They were doing their best to control the large bird, but it was hissing and squawking as it wriggled to escape from their grasp. I ushered them straight into an empty consulting room. There are times when it just isn't right to ask someone to take a seat in the waiting room until the vet is ready to see them.

The women were convinced that the bird had a broken wing. Would I be able to fix it? As I listened to their account, I reflected on the unusual niche swans occupy in our society in the twenty-first century.

Swans are wild birds, yet they are often dependent on humans for survival. Lakes and rivers in areas frequented by the public often have residential swan populations. Indeed, my local town has a small shallow-watered harbour that's home to a flock of over a hundred swans. Children are brought by parents and grandparents to view these semi-domesticated, graceful creatures, and rumours that swans can break a leg with a flapping wing ensure that people never get too close to the birds. This fear of swans is reinforced by the intimidating hiss of an indignant swan if it feels that its personal space has been intruded. Nevertheless, many people like feeding bread to the swans and there's a strong sense of public goodwill towards them, with people keeping an eye on them, spotting if a bird is sick or injured. Whenever a bird suffers an ailment, the local vet is called to help. A lame swan? A bird with a droopy wing? A bird with a grazed webbed foot? These are among the many reasons I've been summoned to the harbour to deal with an ailing swan.

There are few natural predators of adult swans, and most injuries occur following attacks by dogs, road accidents or traumatic injuries after swans have flown into overhead cables. Pollution, such as fishing tackle or oil spills, can also cause problems. Old age is a common issue too. Swans live for around twelve years in the wild, and so it's normal to find sick and dying birds as part of the normal life cycle in a flock of a hundred or more birds.

In recent years, I've worked with local bird enthusiasts to fine-tune the system for treating the birds effectively. We have named the harbour area a 'Swan Sanctuary', and erected notice boards with information about the birds. There's an outline of the history of the bird population, information on the correct way to feed them, and contact numbers to call if a bird is in trouble. We have organised a small network of volunteers who have been trained and equipped as swan 'first-aiders'. If a call comes in about a sick or injured swan, it can be difficult to send a vet down at once, so it's far more efficient to have a bank of trained lay people: one of them is usually available to come down to the harbour and assess the situation.

Sometimes, no intervention is needed: for example, there are a few geriatric swans with chronic lameness. People phone the emergency number because they feel sorry for these birds, but given that they spend most of their lives swimming on the water, they don't need our help. They live pain-free, comfortable lives for the most part, only hobbling awkwardly when they step ashore to feed on the bread thrown to them by locals.

When a swan is genuinely in need of veterinary attention, the volunteers have been trained in how to catch them, using a special 'swan bag' to restrain and carry them; the trussed-up swan is then brought by car to see me. Which is why I was not surprised when the women appeared in my waiting room with that hissing, hooting swan. Their names were Brenda and Marcia; they were the key members of our volunteer swan rescue team and I knew them well.

Once we had the bird in the consulting room, I turned off the light, and in the darkened, enclosed environment, the swan quietened down. I was able to slowly examine him, starting from his beak, working backwards and checking him all over. He had a ring around his leg, with an engraved number which I noted: later, I'd discover from the central register that he was a one-year-old bird who had been ringed by a volunteer 20km away, at a swan colony on local marshlands, where he had presumably originally hatched out.

My examination confirmed Brenda and Marcia's suspicions: the swan's right wing was drooping below his body, and I could tell by feeling along its length that the main upper bone, the humerus, was broken. For a bird, this is disastrous: it's similar to a racehorse fracturing one of the main leg bones. The strength and precision of the bones is critical for normal function: running in the case of the horse, and flying for the swan. While the broken bone could perhaps be surgically repaired, it would need a miracle for this to be done in a way that would allow the bird to fly again. And how could a swan survive without flying?

I explained the situation to the swan-rescue women. The swan must have flown into an overhead cable, fracturing the bone in the collision or the subsequent fall. He'd never fly again. It seemed that the kindest option was to carry out quiet euthanasia.

'Kindest?' Marcia stuttered. 'How is it kind to kill him? I wouldn't want to die if I were him. I'd want someone to try to save me!'

Brenda was equally upset, but she stayed quiet, biting her lip. She had been volunteering with the swans for longer than Marcia, and she knew that the reality of swan rescue wasn't always easy.

I tried to rationalise the situation: there were over a hundred swans in the colony, this bird would struggle to stay healthy if he couldn't fly, he'd be vulnerable to dog attacks, there were many reasons why it could be cruel to keep him alive.

'But surely someone, somewhere can help him,' Marcia carried on.

I never like to dampen enthusiasm and kindness, however much I feel that it may be misguided. I used the speakerphone to call a friend who had helped me with tricky swan cases before, Dorothy Beeson. She runs the Swan Sanctuary in London, which has the only dedicated swan-operating theatre in Europe. When she answered, I explained the background, expecting her to agree with my suggested course of action, but this was a woman who had created a swan sanctuary in her back garden because of her compassion for the birds. As she listened to the story, she could hear Marcia's voice interjecting, so I think she appreciated the subtleties of the situation.

'Pete, I think you're right that the poor bird won't fly again. But if you can get him to our sanctuary, we'll pull out all the stops for him. We'll take the x-rays, get our orthopaedic swan vet to check him out, and we'll do our best to make him fly again. Can you do that?' was her response.

I had a busy waiting room full of delayed appointments, and I was now being asked to transport a badly injured swan across the Irish Sea to London. What was I supposed to do?

'OK, Dot. I'll see what I can do.'

I promised Marcia and Brenda that I would do as Dot suggested, and after giving the bird an injection of pain relief, we moved him into a hospital cage in a dark room. Over lunch, I pondered the problem. Remarkably, it just took one phone call to solve it. I called a newly launched airline that had recently started daily flights to London City Airport. I explained my dilemma: could they help me take the swan to London. The company – Cityjet – responded magnificently. 'Of course we can help. How about a mid-morning flight tomorrow? You'll need to accompany the bird yourself, but if you can do that, we'll fly you both there, and we'll do it for free.'

So the next morning, I found myself in the cargo section of Dublin airport, carrying the swan across the tarmac then up the steps into a smart, shiny new jet. I was asked to sit in one of the front plush leather seats: nothing but business class for this swan. It seemed even odder when glamorous, smartly dressed air hostesses sat down beside the two of us; most people are frightened of swans and don't want to be near them. Moments later, I began to understand what was going on: I could hear a hubbub of chatter approaching, and a small crowd clutching camera equipment came up the gangway. The Cityjet PR department had put the word out, and we had become the focus of an organised photo shoot.

As I did my best to smile for the cameras (not easy with a large indignant bird in my lap), my mobile phone rang. It was the national radio station, with the main morning show wanting to have a word. 'Is it true that Cityjet are flying a swan with a broken wing to London?'

The media circus soon dissipated, the swan and I were moved to a discreet area at the back of the jet, and the flight to London proceeded uneventfully. We were met on the tarmac by Dot with her own team of swan volunteers and a dedicated swan ambulance. I handed our swan over, feeling surprisingly sad to say goodbye, and I returned to Dublin immediately on the same jet.

The following morning, there were two pieces of news over breakfast. First, Dot called: the wing was so badly broken that the orthopaedic vets had decided that the best course of action had been amputation. She had already found an owner of a private lake in Devon who had promised to care for the swan in a safe, hazard-free environment till the end of his days.

Second, I discovered that our flight of mercy had made the front page of the Irish national newspapers. The quirky image of a vet speaking on a mobile phone while sitting in the front row of an aeroplane with a swan on his lap had provided Cityjet with more free advertising than they'd had all summer.

Questions and answers on wild birds and poultry

As a vet, I need to be ready to treat all animals, and that doesn't just mean commonly kept pet birds like parrots and budgies. Wild birds and poultry are just as likely to need veterinary attention. As the Telegraph *vet, I'm often asked questions about such creatures: here are some examples.*

I have a young seagull waiting by my kitchen door morning and evening. It eats leftover cat food that I leave out, but should I be giving it more than this? It can fly in short bursts, from chair to table to hedge to garage roof, when pressed to do so by neighbourhood cats. There is no sign of its parents. Should I be doing anything else and will it ever leave?

GD, Kent

The high-protein content of tinned cat food is ideal for a growing seagull. It sounds as if this bird is well on the way to adulthood, and should soon be able to fly properly. Seagulls are intelligent birds, and they tend to gravitate towards rich sources of food. You may want to reduce the amount of food you are giving once all of his adult feathers are in, if you want him to return to the wild. Perhaps you would like to have a permanent new resident in your garden, but take care

– word may spread in the seagull world, and you could find a small flock of his friends enjoying your hospitality.

> For the past six weeks, the wallpaper in our porch has been 'pecked'. It only happens during the day when our main door is open, and we think it is either a blackbird or a smaller bird. We have lived in our house for twenty years and this has never happened before. Have you any ideas how to prevent it? I have used tin foil on some areas, which does help, but the pecking just moves onto another area. I tried hanging up a bird deterrent (a metal cat face with green marble eyes), but this only worked for a few days.
>
> *NF, East Lothian*

You can choose from a range of different humane bird-deterrent methods, available from websites such as www.birdbusters.com. There is a kit designed to deter woodpeckers from causing damage to buildings that might be the answer. It includes scare balloons, painted with large 'predator' eyes, a fake octopus with dangly plastic tape legs that frighten birds, and special protective spray for the wallpaper that releases a safe but unpleasant taste when pecked. You should also look for reasons why the birds are suddenly so interested in your porch – could there be tiny insects that they are eating?

The hamlet in which I live has been adopted by a wild peacock for the last two years. My neighbours and I have been feeding him with mixed bird seeds, of which sunflower seeds seem to be the favourite. We are wondering if there is any other type of food we should be giving to him for a balanced diet. We are all very fond of him and are concerned for his welfare.

DB, Devon

The peacock must be having a good, varied diet, due to his free-range lifestyle, but you can improve the supplements you give him. Problems commonly occur when a particular food item is repeatedly picked out as a favourite. Sunflower seeds may be tasty, but they have a very high fat level of 40 per cent or more. You should seek out a game bird pellet or crumble, of the type designed to feed pheasants. This has been designed to provide complete nutrition, and your peacock will thrive on it. Get it from your local agricultural merchant.

I've always loved ostriches – from their huge eggs, to feather boas to their cheeky long-necked appearance. I've recently retired, so I have plenty of time on my hands, and I have an acre of meadowland around my house. Would I be completely mad to consider keeping an ostrich as a pet?

PP, Nottinghamshire

In theory it's possible to keep a pet ostrich, but I wouldn't recommend it. They're huge, at 8–10 feet tall, and they can be aggressive (they have a vicious kick as well as a frightening peck). They're expensive to keep – you'd need to have adequate facilities, including fencing and methods of restraint, and you'd need to pay for an annual licence under the Dangerous Wild Animals Act. If you're serious about this, you'd be better to start with an emu (only 5 foot tall) or a rhea (6 foot tall). Neither is on the Dangerous Wild Animals list, so no licence is needed. Their smaller size makes them easier to keep, and they'll still give you huge eggs and feathers. Before you do anything, however, have a long talk with an experienced big-bird keeper. After doing that, I think you'd be likely to conclude that yes, it would be verging on insanity.

18

The dog who learned sign language

Did you know that deafness is linked to white coat colour in both dogs and cats? The case of Maisie is a good example of how this disability can impact on the life of an animal. Sometimes the job of a vet is to help to find ways of dealing with established issues that are troubling pets.

Maisie was a boxer with an unusual coat colour for her breed: she was completely white, apart from a few blotches of black spots around her muzzle. She had clear blue eyes, caused by an absence of pigment, and her all-white coat and pale blue eyes gave her an appealing, almost ghost-like appearance. Unfortunately, her white coat colour was also a marker of a problem that Maisie had probably suffered from since birth: completely deafness in both ears.

Her owner, Fiona, was aware of Maisie's potential deafness before she took her on as a puppy, and part of the agreement with the breeder when she bought her was that she would not show her, nor breed from her, since any deafness caused by a genetic abnormality would be passed down to her puppies if Maisie became a mother.

Coat pigmentation and the colour of the back of the eye are both created by pigment-producing cells, known as 'melanocytes'. If the genes to produce these cells are absent, a white coat and blue eyes are the consequence. Hearing is made possible through a layer of specialised cells in the inner ear. These 'hearing' cells originate from the same stem cells as pigment-producing cells. Therefore if an animal has no pigment in its body, it is likely that it will also be deficient in the specialised 'hearing' cells, and deafness is a common consequence.

If a breeder produces a white puppy or kitten, deafness is high on the list of probabilities, but it can be surprisingly difficult to assess their hearing. Fiona had been told by the dog breeder that Maisie would probably be deaf, but she brought her to me to have a professional review of the situation. She wanted to know if Maisie was definitely deaf, and if so, what could be done to help her. Could she get a hearing aid? What about cochlear implants, as for humans?

The first issue was to try to establish Maisie's hearing ability. It's easy with adult humans: sounds of varying pitches and volumes can be played through headphones, with a button being pressed when the sound is heard. A graph can then be drawn up showing the hearing response throughout the audio spectrum. Even if the button-pressing model isn't used, as soon as children are old enough to talk, they can be asked the simple question, 'Can you hear this?' It's more complicated with animals, perhaps not dissimilar to working with young children.

Many types of tests can be carried out, such as calling the animal's name, knocking on windows, blowing whistles, squeaking toys, ringing bells or spraying aerosol cans. The idea is to create these sounds to the side, or behind, the animal, and to watch for a reaction that indicates that they've heard the sound. The animal might turn towards you, cock the head to one side, or make some other movement that suggests that they've heard. It can sometimes involve a subjective interpretation of whether or not they've heard, and repeated tests are often needed to make a judgement. The possibility of poor hearing, or partial deafness, can make this very complicated.

The other senses of deaf animals sometimes seem to be heightened: they can be very sensitive to vibrations, or have excellent eyesight that allows them to see movement at the fringes of their vision, so you have to be very careful when doing hearing tests to ensure that the only possible reason for a reaction is that the sound has been heard. To add to the complications, young animals with normal hearing some-times ignore sounds, so a lack of response does not prove that they are deaf.

There is a definitive, scientific test for hearing in animals. The so-called Brainstem Auditory Evoked Response (BAER) test involves connecting electrodes up to the skull, and measuring electrical activity in the brain. With normal hearing, electrical spikes of brain activity are seen when a sound is made beside the ear. This test provides a clear, objective way of checking the hearing in one or both ears. Unfortunately, the test is only available at a few specialist centres around the UK, and not in Ireland at all. So while it's useful, it isn't a test that vets use every day in practice.

Maisie was twelve-weeks-old-when I saw her for her hearing assessment. She was a delightful puppy and I could see why Fiona had fallen for her. She oozed good nature and friendliness, wagging her whole body rather than just her tail in her enthusiasm to meet new people. It was difficult to get her to stay still on the consultation table, but after ten minutes of getting to know each other, she began to calm down and settle.

I had prepared a series of noise-making devices, starting with a squeaky dog toy, moving up to an electronic horn (so loud that you'd think it might deafen her if she was not already deaf). Fiona steadied Maisie on the table while I stood behind her, staying still while squeezing the toy and pressing the noise-making button. Maisie didn't flinch or make any movement at all when I made the noises. To test her general level of reactivity, I moved into her field of view, and waved. She immediately turned her head to look at me. If she didn't ignore such activity, it seemed unlikely that she'd ignore a sound. I was now certain that Maisie was profoundly deaf.

Fiona had been expecting this outcome, but she wanted to know what she could do to help her pet have the best possible quality of life.

There's no cure for this type of deafness in animals. Hearing aids, implanted into dogs' ears, have been used in academic studies, but they are only effective if a dog has the basic anatomical elements of hearing in place: they wouldn't work for Maisie. Cochlear implants would theoretically help: these bypass the normal hearing process, replacing the natural inner ear with an electronic sound sensor. They include a microphone and wiring, which detect and transmit a signal to an implanted device in the inner ear, providing artificial stimulation to the cochlear nerve, which passes impulses on to the brain as the sensation of sound. The significant issue with cochlear implants is the cost. At around £20,000 per ear, one can see why they have not caught on in the canine world.

So, given that Maisie was certain to be deaf for her whole life, Fiona wanted to know what could be done to help her.

Deafness has a profound impact on an animal's life, and they have to be protected by their owners throughout their lives to keep them safe. Deaf dogs and cats cannot hear hazards approaching, and are particularly vulnerable to injury, especially from cars, but also from predators or aggressive animals.

Deaf cats need to be indoor-only pets, since there are too many risks if they are allowed to live free-ranging outdoor lives. Dogs don't need such a radical change in lifestyle, since most live in an enclosed area of the home and garden anyway. The main issue is that they can't be allowed off the lead when out in open areas on walks. If they are allowed to run freely, they can't hear their owners calling them back, nor can they hear important sounds of danger, such as oncoming traffic.

I suggested that Fiona buy the longest possible extendible lead, to give Maisie as much freedom as possible. The best type of lead is the stretchy bungee-type lead, which allows flexible, active movement while still letting Fiona to pull her back in a controlled way if needed. The type where a narrow cord spins out from a plastic handle can cut into hands like a cheesewire.

Although Maisie was deaf, her other senses would be likely to compensate by gradually becoming more sensitive than normal. Simple tests in the consult room confirmed that she had excellent vision, and she had an exquisitely delicate sense of touch, turning immediately if someone brushed against her. I also suggested that Fiona should investigate teaching sign language to Maisie. Dogs are intelligent, fast learners, and just as with deaf humans, sign language has become a key way of communicating with deaf animals. For starters, Fiona would be able to train Maisie to obey hand signals instead of verbal commands, for actions such as 'Sit', 'Stay' and 'Lie down'.

Owners of deaf dogs need to learn a range of tricks to make life easier, such as stamping on the ground to get a pet's attention: they can pick up the tremor and it prompts them to look at you for further instructions with hand signals. A vibrating collar is another possibility to improve communications. This works with a remote control, held by the owner. When the button is pressed, the collar vibrates, giving the dog a cue to look at the owner, and they can then carry out the appropriate sign language to pass on a message to the dog.

There are websites and books written about how to live with a deaf dog: once I had confirmed the diagnosis of deafness, I gave Fiona a list of resources, and it was over to her to do her studies and practise this novel form of dog training and interactions.

One interesting side effect of Maisie's deafness was the fact that she went on to develop an unusually delicate sense of smell. She developed a strong aversion to cigarette smoke, wrinkling her button-boxer nose, and whimpering if she detected even a whiff of smoke. If anybody in Fiona's house lit up, she started to bark, and she refused to stop until the cigarette was extinguished. As she matured, Maisie turned out to be an effective cure for smoking in Fiona's household.

Maisie may have been deaf, but she more than made up for her lack of hearing in myriad ways with her larger-than-life presence in Fiona's family life.

Questions and answers on pet senses and sensitivities

Animals share the same senses as humans, with the proviso that they have greater or lesser sensitivity in some ways. And just as we can suffer from issues relating to our senses (such as deafness and blindness), so can pets. Here are some examples from readers who've written to me at The Telegraph.

> My rabbit looks weird: he has one ear up, and one ear down. I'm told that this may be because he's a cross-bred lop-eared rabbit. Can I help in some way to even up his appearance? Could I stiffen the floppy ear in some way to make it stand up? Or could I put a small weight on the other ear to make it flop?
>
> *JP, Basingstoke*

You remind me of some pedigree dog owners who try to 'correct' their dogs's ears by using superglue or hanging weights from ear tips to make them go up, down or whatever the breed standard demands. None of these efforts make any long-term difference. The shape of ears is dictated by the cartilage shell beneath the skin, and it's not easily modified. My advice? Detach yourself from your worries about your rabbit's appearance. He'll be equally happy with his ears, whether they're up, down or in-between. Who cares if he looks a little quirky?

We have a ginger cat called Honey, who has reached the age of seventeen. She seems in good health but she has started a strange habit of miaowing loudly in the early hours of the morning. It sounds as if she is in pain, and she wakes the whole house. When we go to her, she seems to want nothing more than to be allowed out of the kitchen (where she normally sleeps) and onto the end of our bed. Once she has settled there, she remains quiet and peaceful all night. She does this two or three times a week, but strangely, if we try to keep her in our room at bedtime, she wants to go into the kitchen. Why is she doing this, and what can we do to help?

AG, Ballymena

Honey's loud miaowing could be partly due to deafness. Elderly animals often go deaf, which means that they cannot hear their own voices properly. As a result, they vocalise more loudly than when they were young (I know plenty of dog owners who are equally fed up with their loudly barking geriatric dogs). There could be a few contributing factors to other aspects of Honey's odd behaviour. Older cats are prone to a number of diseases that can affect their daily routines. A disease called hyperthyroidism is one example. Affected cats often have high blood pressure that can make them feel agitated in certain situations, with results such as you describe. You should arrange a visit to your local vet for a Geriatric Cat Check-up. This will involve a long discussion with the vet about all of her habits and behaviours, followed by a careful physical examination, plus some blood and urine samples. It is very likely that some underlying problem will be identified, and hopefully, appropriate treatment can then be given.

Our cocker spaniel Freddie, is absolutely mesmerised by wood-burning stoves. He will happily stare for hours at the glass doors with tail wagging, particularly when they are not burning. We joke that they are his surrogate television. What is he seeing and what could the fascination be?

CJ by email

It is fascinating to try to work out how our pets perceive the world. I am waiting with eager anticipation for some computer buff to invent a virtual simulation of the way our pets experience life. Smells would be much stronger, sound would be louder and over a wider frequency range, and vision would be less detailed and less colourful. To understand Freddie's behaviour, perhaps you should get down on all fours, and try to imagine a 'dog's view' of the stove. There may be an interesting smell, and when he looks in the glass, he may see a distorted reflection that he finds intriguing in some way. When the stove is burning, Freddie will hear a range of crackly sounds, and perhaps when it is not in action, he may be curious about the absence of sounds. Many dogs develop minor obsessions about interesting objects. Sticks, stones or cats are a more common focus of attention, and I suspect Freddie's 'television' is a unique and harmless idiosyncrasy.

I heard about a man who gave a sleeping dog a fright by bursting a paper bag beside her head. The following day, the man was snoozing in his armchair, and the dog crept up to him, then barked loudly in his ear. People watching were convinced that the dog was quietly laughing as she walked away from the startled man. Do animals have a sense of humour?

SG, Dublin

It's easy to anthropomorphise, presuming that when animals display certain behaviour, they have human-type thoughts going through their heads. We know that this is often not the case, with animals lacking the type of self-awareness and complex thought processes that humans experience. At the same time, it's arrogant for us humans to presume that we're the only living creatures to enjoy a wide range of emotions including sadness, joy and humour. The truth is that, in the absence of language, we just don't know what goes on inside animals' minds. But you just need to watch dogs playing with each other, or have a cat sitting on your keyboard when you're trying to type, to realise that animals do find some things funny, just as we do.

19

The guide dog for a blind dog

Some pets have seamless, easy lives, sashaying from uneventful youth, through a health-filled adulthood into smooth old age. I meet these animals as puppies and kittens, see them intermittently for routine health checks and vaccinations, then I help them out of their lives at the end of their natural life span. Life is easy not just for these animals and their owners, but also for their vet.

Other dogs, like Ross, battle through life with health challenges from the start, somehow surviving and even thriving, but only with continual input from their owners, and regular visits to the vet to tackle their complex issues. There was no great mystery about Ross's problems, but there were often difficult decisions to make. My role wasn't to make those decisions, but to help his owners weigh the pros and cons, the advantages and disadvantages, and then to support them in their decisions. The puzzle in these animals' lives is not what needs to be done, but whether or not to do it. When is it wiser to stop?

Ross was a rescue dog. He was found wandering around a small town one Christmas Eve and someone took him to a local animal sanctuary. He wasn't microchipped, he didn't have a collar on and nobody came looking for him, so his early life remained unknown.

Soon after, the Martin family visited the sanctuary to get a puppy, only to discover that they were too early for the usual post-Christmas glut of unwanted puppies given as presents. While they were visiting, adult rescue dogs surrounded them, jumping up and down, vying for attention. They had no intention of taking on an adult dog, but then they noticed Ross, a small rough-coated terrier. He had an appealing appearance, with a mostly white coat but light brown fur covering his ears and around his eyes. This gave his face a pleasing symmetry, almost as if he was wearing a brown hat. He was behaving differently, sitting back quietly from the crowds of dogs, staying in his own private space. They discovered why he was so withdrawn: even though he was just a young adult, he was completely blind due to an inherited eye disease, which had caused his retinas to degenerate. His eyes looked normal, but he couldn't see anything. It was no wonder that he felt unable to join in with the melee of rescue dogs: he would have felt vulnerable and frightened. When the Martin family asked what the plan was for Ross, the sanctuary owners hesitated. 'It isn't going to be easy: who wants a young blind dog when there are so many healthy animals that need homes?' The Martin family felt sorry for Ross, and after a hurried discussion, they decided to take him home with them that day.

They discovered almost at once that Ross had learned to cope well with his blindness. He was quiet and withdrawn when he first arrived at a new location, a deliberate strategy to use the time to learn to recognise and memorise his surroundings. He would move slowly around a room, sniffing and feeling with his nose, pressing his side against solid objects on the left and on the right, gradually mapping out the physical structures in the room. Once he'd done this a few times, he grew in confidence, soon being able to move quickly around the room, and eventually moving so much like a normal dog that visitors wouldn't realise that he was blind. Ross soon became a much-loved member of their family.

I grew to know him well: the Martins were conscious of his vulnerabilities as a blind dog, and they made sure to bring him to see me at least twice a year, just to check that all was well. Vision aside, he was a healthy, fit dog who enjoyed life. His blindness never seemed to bother him; he adapted, using his senses of smell, hearing and touch. He walked from side to side, in a zig-zag, as if he'd learned that this was the best way to avoid full-on collisions with objects. At home, he knew the geography of the rooms so well that he ran around like a dog with normal sight. The Martin family knew that they had to be careful about changing the layout of a room and to keep the house tidy, putting toys and other objects away so that Ross wouldn't bump into them.

Ross did escape from home on a couple of occasions; he still had the curious, exploring instincts of a terrier, and a door just had to be left open with a crack for Ross to sense the fresh air and make a dash for it. These escape incidents caused chaos and panic. Everyone knew that he'd be a liability in traffic, risking his own life as well as that of pedestrians and others, as cars swerved to avoid him. He somehow survived this danger each time, but he got utterly lost, as there was no way that he could find his own way home. Blind dogs are rare in a small town, and he was returned safely each time, but soon the family securely fenced in their front and back gardens: if Ross did get outside, he now could go no further than the end of the garden.

Dogs are social creatures, and Ross was no different to a normally sighted dog in this way. The Martins took on a new puppy soon after Ross arrived, a cross bred King Charles spaniel/West Highland white terrier named Silky. The two dogs became friends at once, and almost miraculously, Silky fell into the role of being Ross's 'seeing eyes' when they were out on walks. She would trot along just in front of him, and if he fell behind, she noticed, and came back for him. He followed close behind her, learning how to shadow her closely without being in direct contact. The routine allowed him to be much more adventurous than if he had been on his own, similar to the way a blind human para-athlete uses a guide runner or cyclist to allow them to move at speed.

Ross loved his walks, getting as excited about them beforehand as any dog. He used to sniff the air more than dogs with normal sight, and his favourite walk was the beach, where he learned that he could charge around at speed, even without Silky, because there was nothing at all for him to bump into.

As if being blind was not bad enough, as time passed, Ross began to develop physical problems with his sightless eyes. First he developed cataracts. The internal anatomy of both eyes had been distorted by the hereditary problem that had caused his initial blindness. As a result, the normal structure of the lens in each eye began to suffer from premature aging. A healthy lens is completely translucent, like clear glass. If the protein in the lens degenerates, this clarity is disturbed, with the lens changing to a milky blue-white colour. If a dog has otherwise normally healthy eyes, the opacity of cataracts obscures their vision, and they gradually become blind. Cataract surgery, where the opaque lenses are surgically removed, is often carried out in these cases, and blind dogs are able to see again. In Ross's case, there was no point in removing the cataracts, since he was already blind because of the changes in his retinas. As it was, his eyes now looked abnormal, with milky-white centres rather than the black pupils of healthy eyes. But otherwise, life continued as usual for Ross.

The next complication for Ross was more serious. As the cataracts matured in his lenses, they began to swell. A normal lens is held in the centre of the eye by fibrous ligaments, like the elastic cords that support a circular trampoline inside its frame. As the diseased lenses began to swell, these ligaments tore, and without their support, the cataracts slipped out of their central position in the eyes. They became mobile, like elliptical ball bearings bouncing around inside his eyes. Ross began to suffer serious pain and the pressure inside his eyes increased because of the inflammation. He became a quiet, reserved dog because of the continual pain in his eyes.

There was only one way to deal with this pain: to remove both eyes. This was a difficult decision for the Martins. It was one thing to have a blind dog with eyes, but it seemed different to consider putting a dog through surgery to cut his eyes out. Was it fair to do this? After all Ross had been through, was this a sign that he had finally had enough? They knew from talking to their neighbours that some people felt that it would be kinder to carry out gentle euthanasia, bringing his difficult life to a peaceful end.

The Martins came to me to have a rational, calm discussion about the choice. They knew he'd look odd with no eyes, but they also realised that he couldn't see anyway. As far as Ross was concerned, his eyes had become a painful nuisance and he'd be happier without them. When they thought about the situation from Ross's perspective, it seemed obvious that removing his eyes was a positive step rather than something to be feared or avoided.

The surgery to remove his eyes went smoothly, and almost immediately, Ross was like a different dog. He became more active, more lively and he started to engage with people and animals again. With hindsight, the Martins realised that the discomfort of his eyes had been troubling Ross for some time. They had thought he was just getting old and quiet; the truth was that he had been suffering from chronic, low-grade ocular pain.

They never regretted the decision to remove his eyes. Ross was now completely pain-free and comfortable. He went on to be a calm, relaxed and friendly dog for many more years. When the Martins were asked to describe his personality, they'd say he was 'always happy', and 'a thorough gentleman'. He was content to be just as he was, alive and at ease with life and his environment.

Ross, the sightless, eyeless, but happy little dog, lived as long as any healthy dog could. The Martins brought him to me finally after they'd had him for fifteen years; we estimated he was then seventeen years old. He had been slowing up for a while, and for the previous two mornings he had refused to get out of his bed and hadn't wanted to eat. They decided that this was a sign that he had had enough of life. He was peaceful and calm during his final visit. The Martins crowded around, each with a hand on their beloved Ross as he put his head down to rest. He'd had an inspiring life, and he'd left them with memories to treasure. And he'd taught his vet an important lesson: how life can be enjoyed by animals even when they're faced with seemingly monumental difficulties.

Questions and answers on pet eyes and vision

Eyes are sensitive structures: they express an animal's personality and moods, as well as providing the special sense of vision. Owners naturally worry when their pets' eyes are not in full health. I have often answered readers' questions about issues affecting eyes and vision.

> My four-year-old blue roan cocker spaniel has developed a small round opaque spot on each eye. My vet has suggested that the eye spot is cholesterol due to obesity and that I over-feed her. She is definitely overweight, but I don't feed her much – only a weighed amount every day, with no snacks – and she's taken for plenty of good walks. Can the spots be treated effectively?
>
> *MP, Brittany*

Small fatty – or cholesterol – deposits in the front of the eyes are common in young and middle-aged dogs, and there's often (but not always) an association with high levels of fats circulating in the bloodstream. This can be caused by some hormonal diseases that need treatment (such as an underactive thyroid gland) and it could be worth discussing this possibility with your vet. You should also ask about an ultra-low-fat diet, such as the Hills r/d Prescription Diet®, to lower the level of fat in the bloodstream, which may reduce the risk of these spots getting larger. The spots do not usually cause blindness – dogs are able to 'see around them' – but they do need to be monitored carefully.

My daughter's eight-month-old female cat Jemima has just been diagnosed by the vet as having lost her sight in both eyes – she has detached retinas. She does not appear to be able to make any differentiation between dark and light and is very wary of moving around, even in familiar territory. The vet has suggested that she should be kept inside, but we would prefer her to be able to lead as normal a life as possible. Have you any suggestions about how to keep Jemima safe but also to allow her as much freedom as possible in the circumstances?

PC, Brighton

Cats that lose their vision gradually, or that are born with blindness, tend to cope better compared to those that become blind very rapidly, like Jemima. You need to allow her plenty of time to get used to her new world. At first, you should confine her to one or two safe and familiar rooms when you are not around to keep an eye on her. You should get her used to wearing a body harness with a lead, so that you can supervise her carefully as you gradually let her experience more of the world. I do know of owners who allow blind cats complete freedom to come and go outside, but this involves a high level of risk (from other animals, traffic hazards and other physical dangers). Jemima will have to live a life of freedom only within carefully defined areas that you know are safe for her.

> Our twenty-year-old blue Burmese cat, Misty, has a curious visual defect. At night in artificial light she is unable to see anything, walks into the furniture and cannot find her way about. When we greet her in the morning in natural light her vision has returned and she jumps onto the table for her food and can see everything. This trouble happens every night and we notice her pupils are dilated when she can't see. What do you think the cause of this could be?
>
> *AB, Norfolk*

If you used a photographic light meter to measure light levels, you'd find that it's much brighter in the morning, with natural light, compared to the evenings, with only artificial light. You're being fooled by your own eyes' adaptation to differing light levels, so that the light levels seem similar to you. It sounds as if Misty is in the early stages of blindness: the problem is always first apparent at night-time. Her pupils are dilated due to a reflex that's attempting to let as much light into the back of the eye as possible. Older cats commonly develop disease of the retina secondary to high blood pressure, a problem that can be successfully treated. You should take her to a vet to have a thorough eye examination and blood pressure measurement, and if you're lucky, you may be able to nip this problem in the bud.

> Babe, my two-year-old female guinea pig, has a cataract in her right eye. Her left eye looks normal. What could have caused this, and is there anything I can do about it? She must be blind in that eye, but doesn't seem bothered about it at all.
>
> *DN by email*

Cataracts are sometimes hereditary in guinea pigs, but they can also be caused by diabetes, and by trauma (e.g. bashing the side of her head). It's worth asking your vet to check her blood glucose to rule out diabetes. I've never had to treat a diabetic guinea pig, but there are plenty of cases reported in the literature. They can often be helped by simply adjusting the diet, although tiny injections of insulin are sometimes needed. In theory, the cataract could be removed by a veterinary eye specialist, but most people would find it difficult to justify the high cost of the operation (especially if she has good vision in her other eye).

20

The playful cat who stopped playing

Cookie had always been an exceptionally playful cat. I first met him when he was a kitten, a black-and-white bundle of fluff and energy. His fur seemed to stand up on end, almost as though he had a frizzy halo around his body. As I tried to examine him, he kept trying to bat my stethoscope with his paws. Later on, he spent a day with us when he was neutered, and as soon as he had recovered from his anaesthetic, he was at the front of his cage, reaching out to pat anybody who walked past. His owner, Jackie, told me that he was the same at home. He just loved playing with anything that was within reach.

Jackie bought a multitude of toys for him, including wands with dangling feathers, electric mice that darted around the floor and laser light beams that encouraged him to chase a bright dot of light. In fact, there was no need for her to buy him toys: homemade games were just as much fun. If she rolled up a piece of paper and threw it across the room, he'd chase it and bring it back to be thrown again. Jackie is an embroidery, knitting and patchwork enthusiast, and she'd often have balls of wool around: if Cookie was able to grab one, he'd spend hours chasing it around the floor while it gradually unravelled.

One day, for no apparent reason, Cookie stopped playing. He woke up one morning, looked around at his usual toys, and went back to sleep. Jackie didn't worry about this at first: perhaps he had played late the night before, and was tired. But he kept sleeping all morning, and at lunchtime, when he was normally chasing a ball around the kitchen floor while she prepared food, he was still sleeping. When Jackie talked to him, he seemed responsive enough, purring and pressing his head against her hand, but that was it. As soon as she moved away, he curled up to sleep some more. It was his refusal to eat that prompted Jackie to bring him to see me. Cookie had always been a regular grazer: he'd eaten breakfast, lunch and dinner, every day since he was a kitten, but on this non-playing day, he didn't even look at his bowl in the morning, and at lunchtime, when Jackie pushed some chopped roast chicken (his favourite) under his nose, he turned his head away. At this stage, Jackie knew there was something wrong with him, so she lifted him into his cat carrier and came down to my clinic.

I was always pleased to see Cookie: he was an unusually pleasant and friendly animal. Even on this occasion, he lifted his head up, looked at me and purred when the top of his carrier was opened. I lifted him out, speaking to him as I examined him, and he continued to purr. I checked him carefully all over, going through my usual clinical examination, but I couldn't find anything wrong. Cookie was such a confirmed creature of habit that it was just not possible that he could be having an 'off' day for a simple, harmless reason. Jackie was very clear that she knew that there was something troubling him, and I agreed with her. The big question was 'what?'

This was one of those occasions when I would have loved my patient to be able to talk to me. I had no doubt that Cookie knew that there was something wrong, and if he could communicate, he would say something like 'I have a headache', or 'My tummy's sore' or 'I have a tight feeling in my chest'. As it was, he just looked at me and purred, curling up to sleep when I put him back in his carrier.

The only way forward was to carry out a detailed investigation to look for the reason for his changed behaviour. I started with a blood sample: within twenty minutes, our practice laboratory had confirmed that Cookie's internal metabolism was functioning normally, with no sign of liver, kidney or other internal disease. His blood count was normal too, ruling out major internal inflammation or tissue damage. This was all good news, but it didn't take us any closer to making a diagnosis.

The next step was radiography: I sedated Cookie to take x-ray pictures of his chest and abdomen. Again, everything was normal, with no clues to suggest what might be wrong with him. At this point, I did what I do when faced with complicated cases that don't seem to make sense. I sat in front of my computer in a quiet, dimly lit room and wrote a detailed account of every tiny feature of Cookie's problem. I then stared at it, thinking through the possibilities. Sometimes when I do this, an idea pops into my head. I've heard musicians say that sometimes lyrics and tunes seem to just arrive in their minds, fully formed. I'm convinced that there is a veterinary equivalent of this in some cases: a sudden thought that makes sense of a complex case just 'happens'.

There are many, many other times when this sudden inspiration doesn't happen. In such cases, I use my written case summary for another purpose: I email it to an online veterinary community that's been set up to help. Veterinary Information Networks (www.vin.com) is a subscription service for vets: we pay a monthly fee to join a group of over 30,000 vets around the world. I can share the details of any baffling cases with this community. Specialists are paid to scrutinise such cases, offering feedback and suggestions. The community is primarily based in North America, which runs five to eight hours behind my time zone, so if I submit a case at the end of my working day, I am almost guaranteed to have an answer in my inbox by breakfast the following morning. The service allows easy sharing of all case details: as well as the vet's written thoughts and findings, this includes blood results, x-ray pictures, ultrasound videos, and of course, normal photographs and videos.

As it happened, VIN wasn't needed to help me with Cookie. As I sat there, writing down his story, one of those sudden inspiring thoughts came to me. I had proven that Cookie's body and metabolism was fundamentally healthy. He was still a cheerful, purring cat. The main issue was that he refused to eat, and that he was duller than normal. Although he had allowed me to examine him carefully, the one area that's always difficult to check out in detail is the back of an animal's mouth. Understandably, pets, even friendly animals like Cookie, don't like it when you open their mouth and try to peer deep inside.

And there's a difference between animals and humans when it comes to oral examinations. When you visit the doctor, you are asked to say 'Ahhhh' so your tongue flattens down and moves forwards, allowing the doctor to view your throat clearly. It isn't possible to get animals to do this, and if you do try to flatten their tongue manually with your finger or an instrument, they don't like it at all. The only way to properly examine the back of the mouth of most animals is when they are anaesthetised, or under sedation.

Cookie was still under sedation following the x-rays, so I quickly went to his kennel, where the nurse was keeping an eye on him. I asked her to help me gently lift his head, and I used a combination of a bright pen torch and a wooden spatula to carefully inspect the back of his tongue and the hidden part of his oral cavity.

I nearly missed it, but once I had spotted it, it was obvious. A fine, narrow translucent piece of thread was wrapped around the base of Cookie's tongue. I could see the end of the thread trailing backwards, to the back of his mouth, and beyond. When I pulled on the thread, it would not move: the object was lodged somewhere further down his digestive tract.

Now I knew what had happened. Cookie had been playing with one of Jackie's hobby objects, and had somehow managed to swallow it. The piece of thread had been attached, and now his mouth and throat were trussed up. It must have felt odd and uncomfortable; no wonder he didn't want to eat or play. I tugged gently on the thread that trailed down into his gullet, but it did not budge. Whatever it was attached to was too far down his throat to come back easily.

The way forwards was clear now. I deepened Cookie's sedation to general anaesthesia, and introduced a fibre optic endoscope (a flexible tube with a glass fibre core that I can peer through) to the back of his mouth, gently pushing it down into the oesophagus. As I did this, I could see the translucent thread beside the tip of my endoscope. I followed it along and downwards. Soon, I could see the opening of the stomach ahead of me, and as I pushed the endoscope tip into this, I saw what I was looking for. The thread was attached to a small circle of felt-like material, sitting in Cookie's stomach. It was just big enough to get stuck at the entrance of the stomach as the thread was tugged from his mouth. And the tension between the thread wrapped around his tongue and the object in his stomach was more than enough to stop him wanting to eat.

I introduced a grabbing forceps device into the stomach through the endoscope, and used it to grasp the piece of material. As I pulled it firmly, I was able to draw it back up the oesophagus, and out through Cookie's mouth. I then un-looped the thread from Cookie's tongue and the job was done. I was confident that I had cured Cookie's problem.

As if to prove this, as soon as Cookie woke up from sedation, he miaowed loudly: I took the cue and offered him a small dish of bland food, and he hungrily tucked into it.

When Jackie called to collect Cookie a few hours later, she immediately recognised the thread and felt scrap: 'I wondered where that had gone!'

Since the episode, Cookie has continued to play as often as before, but with one difference: Jackie carefully stores her threads and materials out of his reach, and Cookie has his own toy cupboard, full of real cat toys. And Jackie keeps an inventory: from now on, if a toy goes missing, Jackie wants to know about it from the start.

Questions and answers on pet eating habits

Pets may not suffer from human-style eating disorders, but a good healthy appetite is one of the key indicators of good health. If a pet stops eating, or starts to eat in an odd way, it can be baffling and worrying. Here are some of the questions on this topic that I've answered for readers.

> Three days after I purchased a twelve-week-old male Persian kitten, he stopped eating, and developed a runny nose and a sore tongue. The vet said that he had cat flu and that he'd always carry the virus from now on. He obviously had this while with the breeder although he had been vaccinated twice. I have a three-year-old cat and I am worried that she will catch the virus from him. What can I do to help the kitten and prevent my other cat from catching it?
>
> *LO by email*

Cat flu-virus infection often stops affected cats from eating when they're acutely infected, and it's very common, especially in multiple cat households. It can be impossible for breeders to clear it out completely. Vaccines against cat flu don't prevent the infection, but they do boost the immune system and so prevent serious disease. Infected kittens may carry the virus for life, but they only show signs of illness from time to time, especially if they're stressed for any reason. (There are similarities with herpes virus cold sores in humans.) Talk to your vet about giving the kitten a daily food supplement of lysine (an amino acid). This can help to prevent flare-ups and may minimise signs of illness. The risk of severe disease in your adult cat is small, provided she's up to date with her vaccines, and is otherwise healthy.

> My young cat is eight months old, and appears to have fur balls. Well, this is the diagnosis I have made. He coughs and retches for minute, sometimes once a day, sometimes more. It is a deep guttural cough that takes over his whole body. He stops eating for a day after doing this then returns to normal. What can I do to help him?
>
> BC, Dublin

You could try giving him a regular dietary lubricant, contained in fur-ball remedies sold by vets or in pet shops. Regular grooming to remove loose hair is also a good idea. You can also get special 'hairball diets', containing high levels of fibre, that have been demonstrated to increase the quantity of hair passing smoothly through the digestive system. Hairballs as a cause of gastrointestinal symptoms in cats may be over-diagnosed. There are often other problems such as dietary allergy or worms that can cause similar signs. I would also give him a broad-spectrum worm dose and try him on a different diet to rule these out.

> My thirteen-year-old Lakeland Terrier has become indifferent to food. Tests at a local referral vet centre show gall bladder problems, which are being treated, but she won't eat. I've tried everything – fish, meat and eggs. Is there anything I can do to stimulate her appetite?
>
> *BL, Liverpool*

Scent is a great appetite stimulant. Try strong-smelling foodstuffs, such as sardines or richly scented fresh meat, and warm it up so it produces an even stronger odour. Dog gravy (e.g. www.waggfoods.com) may improve palatability. Talk to your vet about tasty high-energy semi-liquid diets that you can feed her using a large wide-nozzled syringe. Once she gets the taste via the syringe she may start to eat by herself.

> Our two-year-old springer spaniel carries mouthfuls of food from the kitchen (where he's fed in a bowl) into the living room. He drops the food from his mouth onto the carpet and then eats it. Can you tell me why?
>
> *SB, Cambridge*

This is common. It's an instinctive urge inherited from wild dogs, which evolved to take food away from the primary source to a quieter spot for two reasons: to move away from competition from other dogs in the pack, and to hide from larger predators who might steal their food and threaten them. Sounds like you need to shut the kitchen door!

21

The giant turtle with a tiny appetite

When people visit the vet, they sometimes bring along more than one pet. Most people live busy lives, so it can make sense to deal with several pet problems at the same time. I knew that Marc had brought two pets along, and the first one was straightforward. Mr Bully was a lean, tan-coloured miniature English bull terrier, one of the most amiable creatures to visit my clinic. He needed his annual health check, and he was in shiny good health, so it was a pleasant consultation. Once we'd finished, Marc said casually 'Can I just bring Mr Swampy in?'

'Yes, please do,' I replied, as I finished writing up Mr Bully's case notes. I presumed that Mr Swampy was one of Marc's other dogs; he had a few, and it was sometimes difficult to keep track of their names.

After ten minutes, there was no sign of Marc, so I went out to the car park to see where he was; sometimes people need a hand to get their dogs out of the car. Marc was halfway from the car to the clinic door, with Mr Swampy walking slowly beside him. There was a good reason for his pet to move so slowly, but it left me flabbergasted: Mr Swampy was a giant turtle. His huge shell measured more than half a metre in diameter, and he weighed over 25kg, as much as a golden retriever.

Marc smiled when he saw my obvious astonishment: 'I really should have warned you, shouldn't I?'

It took ten more minutes for Mr Swampy to lumber in through the clinic door and into my consultation room. While we dawdled beside this large slow creature, Marc explained the background to his pet, and the reason for his visit.

Marc didn't set out to get himself a turtle as big as a large dog. He had successfully owned terrapins for several years when someone he knew came across a tiny baby turtle that needed a home. Marc agreed to adopt him, and so Mr Swampy was left on his doorstep in a bucket. At the time, he measured the size of the face of a wristwatch: nobody had an inkling that he was going to get much bigger.

That had been ten years ago. Marc cared for him in the same way as his terrapins, and the only difference was that Mr Swampy didn't just thrive: he flourished, growing bigger and bigger every month like Alfie the tortoise in Roald Dahl's story *Esio Trot*.

When it became obvious that something extraordinary was happening, Marc took photos and measurements of his new pet, and did some research. He discovered Mr Swampy was an American species, the common snapping turtle. Marc was taken aback to discover that Mr Swampy was going to keep growing for twenty years, and he would live for over a hundred years. He was going to be Marc's companion for life.

Mr Swampy soon outgrew the terrapin tank in Marc's living room, and had to be moved into a large heated 2 by 3m tank, in a specially constructed cabin in Marc's back garden. He'd become an active creature who loved swimming, and his high-protein diet consisted of a mixture of fresh meat and fish, including turkey breasts, whole salmon, trout and prawns.

It would be idyllic if Mr Swampy was a benign, friendly gentle giant. In fact, he has become a dangerous, frightening monster. Common snapping turtles are well named: as they grow bigger, they develop long muscular necks, and they can lash out with their jaws with the speed of a striking rattlesnake. Mr Swampy does not have teeth, which is just as well. He once snapped at Marc, catching his hand between his jaws, and it took several weeks for the serious bruising to settle down. Marc respects and admires him, but he isn't a pet who can be cuddled. Mr Swampy enjoys being left to do his own thing, and if he needs to be handled, Marc has learned to approach him from behind, grasping his shell far enough back so that he's safely out of reach of those powerful crushing jaws. Mr Swampy is fortunate to have found an owner like Marc: many other people would have given up the expensive and time-consuming burden of caring for him.

Mr Swampy has always hibernated in the winter, from the beginning of November through until April, but as the climate has become milder in recent years, he's been taking shorter hibernations. He used to snooze for three or four months, but in this particular year, he had only hibernated for two months, waking up at the beginning of January.

The transition from hibernation to normal life is always a stressful time for turtles and tortoises, and it generally takes Mr Swampy a few weeks to get back to his normal eating habits. Marc had brought him to see me because Mr Swampy was struggling to return to full health after his hibernation. His hunger had not returned to its normal enthusiastic level, and Marc had noticed that he had been losing weight. He was now about 10 per cent lighter than he had been at the end of his hibernation.

As Marc lifted the giant reptile onto my consultation table, my first reaction was to suggest that he should take him to a vet with a particular interest in turtles. As a vet in general practice, it's rare for me to see a dinosaur-like creature like Mr Swampy. I knew the basics of reptile care, and although he was far bigger than most of the similar animals that I'd seen in the past, his metabolism would be similar enough to a smaller turtle. But when it came to complex diseases, I felt that I'd quickly be out of my depth. Marc understood my predicament, but he insisted that he'd like me to do an initial assessment, and if needed at a later stage, he'd take him on somewhere else for more specialist intervention. I agreed to see what I could do. The truth was that I was happy to help: I love working with remarkable animals like Mr Swampy.

First, I gave him a careful physical examination. This is difficult to do when an animal is hidden inside a shell, and you're trying to dodge a snapping mouth, but as far as I could tell, his body seemed in good general condition. Secondly, I took an x-ray of his entire body: Mr Swampy was happy to sit still on the x-ray cassette while I lined up the x-ray machine overhead. I could see his lungs on the resulting x-ray picture, and it showed more greyness on one side, with white cloudy patches.

The third part of the investigative process was a blood sample. Collecting blood from a turtle might seem like trying to get blood from a stone, but it's surprisingly easy. Mark lifted Mr Swampy's stubby tail vertically, and I inserted a needle into the midline on the underside of his tail. Blood flowed swiftly into the syringe and in a moment I had enough for a full biochemical and blood cell analysis.

The test results clarified Mr Swampy's problem: he had a raised white blood cell count as well as elevated liver enzymes. The sequence of events was now clear: a turtle's body endures significant stress during hibernation. The complete deprivation of food for a period of months means that the metabolism has to derive energy from body reserves, using novel biochemical pathways. Then, when the animal wakes, the old system of sourcing energy from food via the digestive tract has to be reactivated. These transitions can be challenging for the body, and some turtles need to be fed via a tube after waking to help their bodies readapt to normal nutrition.

It would be highly challenging to introduce a feeding tube through the snapping jaws of Mr Swampy, so I was relieved that he was at least eating something. We could skip that stage. His problem was that on top of the stress to his liver caused by the metabolic transition, he had also picked up pneumonia; this was the reason for his cloudy lungs and the raised white cell count.

There were three strands to his treatment. First, a course of antibiotics given by daily injection would battle the pneumonia. Second, a once-weekly multivitamin injection would help his liver cope with this stressful period. And third, some special dietary supplements would provide his liver with easily digested, highly nutritious support.

Marc was able to give the injections himself, so I didn't see Mr Swampy for another month. Marc had already told me that he had started to eat with more enthusiasm, so this was just a quick check for reassurance. The most significant part of this visit involved placing him on our electronic walk-on scales. He had gained 2kg in weight, which told us that his metabolism had kicked back into normal mode. A repeat blood sample confirmed this wellness: his white cell count and his liver enzymes had returned to normal. While he was at the clinic, we also took a repeat x-ray, and again, there was good news. The clouds on his lungs had cleared.

Marc was delighted that Mr Swampy had made a full recovery, and he only had one concern remaining: the turtle looked as if he was going to have another growth spurt. He's already outgrown the warm tub in the back garden, and Marc's going to have to invest in a newer, bigger version. Marc now reckons that a giant common snapping turtle is the twenty-first-century version of that ancient Thai creature, the white elephant. Does anyone want one?

Questions and answers on reptiles

Reptiles like Mr Swampy add a note of variety to the life of vets, and that includes vets who write newspaper columns. Here's a selection of the reptile-related queries that have come in to me at The Daily Telegraph.

> My iguana lives in a vivarium, but I often let him out to roam around the house. A visitor recently got a nasty fright when he scuttled across the room beside her (he's four feet long). Afterwards she wrote a note to me saying that I might be breaking the law because it's bad for his welfare to be out of his vivarium. Is this true?
>
> *FC by email*

It is true that under the Animal Welfare Act, all owners have an obligation to fulfil their pets' welfare needs, including somewhere suitable to live, a proper diet (including fresh water), the ability to express normal behaviour, any need to be housed with, or apart from, other animals, and protection from, and treatment of, illness and injury. As long as you are meeting these needs, you are not breaking any law, and I don't see that letting him out of his vivarium as you describe need cause any problem. Many reptile owners, however, do accidentally break the law because they are not aware of the correct way of looking after their pets, and many reptiles suffer because of poor husbandry. I'd ask all owners of exotic animals to carry out basic research (e.g. on the internet) to ensure that they have a good understanding of the needs of their pets.

We enjoy walking in the Lake District with Lucy our black Labrador. On a recent and very popular walk near Kendal, Cumbria we came across an adder, basking in the sun across the width of a narrow part of the path. We left it alone but what action should we have taken if our dog had been bitten, given that we were far away from our car and help?

TC by email

The ill effects of the bite of an adder depend on the size of the animal and the area bitten. It can be fatal to a small terrier, but for a Labrador, it's more likely just to be painful. If any animal suffers from a snake bite, don't try anything fancy like sucking out the poison or applying tourniquets. Instead, you need to somehow transport the animal to the nearest vet as rapidly as possible. Many vets in areas where adders are common stock the specific anti-serum that will help to counter the effects of the snake bite. Pain relief and other anti-inflammatory medication will also help to reduce the effects of the toxin.

I am planning to stay with my sister for a month. My only problem is that her daughter had a pet corn snake that escaped from its tank six months ago. I am terrified of snakes and the thought of it emerging from beneath the floorboards into my bedroom is enough to make me break into a sweat. Could the snake have survived, and is this a real possibility?

JW, Shropshire

Some snakes have a remarkable ability to survive for long periods without food: they have been known to live for as long as two years without eating, using biological mechanisms that are not fully understood, including depressing their resting metabolic energy consumption by over 70 per cent. Having said that, most young corn snakes that escape for more than a few days are never seen again, with their fate remaining a mystery. There are many possible outcomes, from being preyed upon by dogs or cats, dying in cold weather outside, or suffering fatal accidents. The risk of a snake encounter is minimal: even if it survived, the snake would do its best to avoid you. Remember that corn snakes are completely harmless anyway, although I realise that this is small consolation to someone who suffers from ophiophobia.

My nine-year-old tortoise has started attacking feet, slippers and shoes when we let her out of her vivarium. She came running into the room the other day and bit my eighteen-month-old daughter's heel. Why is she doing this and how can I stop her?

CF by email

Tortoises can be cute, but they require a more specialised level of care than most owners realise. If her physical and psychological needs are not being properly met (housing, feeding, socialising, toys etc.), this type of bizarre behaviour is more likely to happen. Check with experts to make sure that you are caring for her properly: visit the Tortoise Trust (www.tortoisetrust.org), the British Association of Tortoise Keepers (www.batk.org.uk) and the British Chelonia Group (www.britishcheloniagroup.org.uk). In the meantime, keep her shut up in her vivarium: even a bite from a small tortoise can cause serious problems for a young child.

Every winter we bring our terrapins and fish in from the garden pond to a large tank inside the house. When we feed them, sometimes the terrapins bite the fishes' fins and tails. The wounds do heal with time, but would this hurt the fish? Apart from separating them, what can we do?

JT by email

Would it hurt you if you were bitten by a dog? The pain receptor nervous system of fish is surprisingly similar to our own, so yes, it does hurt the fish to be bitten by the terrapins. Terrapins and fish should not be kept in the same tank or pond; terrapins are omnivores, and small fish are their natural prey. You're lucky that your fish have got away so far with merely being bitten rather than eaten up and swallowed. The outdoor pond may be big enough for the two species to co-exist without problems, but in future, the terrapins will need their own, separate, heated tank for the winter months. You'll find useful care sheets about terrapins at www.britishcheloniagroup.org.uk.

22

The budgies with itchy beaks

The word 'budgerigar' is a bit of a mouthful, and it's no wonder that we shorten the word to 'budgie' for day-to-day use. There is an urban myth that the word 'budgerigar' has its origins from an Australian Aboriginal word meaning 'tasty food'. There may be some truth in this: budgies do originate from Australia, where they can still be seen flying in large colourful groups in the wild. When you've seen the birds enjoying the social life of flocks in the wild, it's sad to see solitary birds in cages, as they're often kept today. Modern pet budgies are bred in captivity, and have never known freedom like their wild ancestors, but there's a strong argument that they should only ever be kept in pairs or small groups. Perhaps the exception to this rule is when an elderly or housebound person keeps a budgie as a continual companion, talking to them and treating them like a close friend. Solitary budgies in this type of set up may relate more closely with their human companions, because they have no other social outlet, and such situations can work well for both human and bird.

Whether alone, in pairs or in small groups, budgies are intelligent little birds, with strong personalities. Stephen, a family man in his forties, bought one bird, a brightly plumaged yellow budgie named Flutter, first. He soon felt sorry seeing her alone in her cage, so four months later, he bought a bigger cage and a second bird, a blue-and-white female called Flap. The two young female budgies seemed to enjoy living in their new large cage together: they cheeped noisily at one another, fluttering around the cage as they interacted. Stephen had the usual budgie 'furniture' in the cage – a mirror, a mini-trapeze and a few perches. He also supplied a cuttlefish bone as a mineral supplement.

At first, both birds seemed to be very healthy, but after a few weeks, Stephen noticed Flap repeatedly scraping her beak against the cuttlefish bone. She seemed to be doing this far more often than Flutter, and when Stephen watched her carefully, he noticed that she seemed to be rubbing her beak on the bars of the side of the cage as well. When Stephen looked closely at Flap's beak, the base of it appeared odd. The normal bright, shiny, polished structure had become dull, and it had a swollen, knobbly appearance. Flap seemed very healthy in every other way: she was eating well, her feathers were bright and colourful, and she was as busy as ever interacting with Flutter. They sat opposite one another on the perch, preening each other's head and neck feathers, chirruping happily.

Stephen first tried a simple pet-shop remedy for beak diseases, but Flap didn't get any better. When Flutter, his original bird, also started scraping her beak against the edge of the cage, Stephen decided to bring both budgies to see me. He transferred them in Flutter's original standard budgie cage for the journey: their aviary-sized enclosure was too big to fit into his car.

I enjoy seeing budgies as patients: they present a different challenge to dogs, cats and other creatures. Budgies are not generally used to being handled, so I do as much as I can from a distance, to avoid upsetting them. As with other animals, the owner's account of what's been happening often provides helpful clues about the issue affecting the pet, so I listened with interest, taking notes, as Stephen explained the background to his two pets.

I then examined both birds carefully without touching them. As I often do these days, I used a digital camera to take a photograph of the affected part of their body: in this case, their beaks. I could then enlarge the image, obtaining as clear a view of the structure as if I was holding each bird in my hand, examining the beak with a magnifying glass. I could see that instead of a healthy, shiny, polished appearance, their beaks had a rough, dull texture. It was as if somebody had taken a piece of sandpaper and rubbed each beak to deliberately coarsen the surface.

There are a few possible causes of beak disease, and as with any medical condition, making the correct diagnosis is essential. In Flap's case, that meant collecting a few fragments of her diseased beak for examination under the microscope. She did not appreciate being handled for this procedure: I darkened the room to make it easier to grasp her in her cage, then Stephen had to hold her still while I used a pair of forceps to nibble away a few scab-like pieces from the base of her beak. Flap was not used to being held in a human hand, and she objected in every way that she could. She is a small bird, but she has a loud screech, and she also has a fierce bite. She grabbed the soft part of Stephen's thumb at the base of his nail, hanging on tightly. I am sure it was very painful for Stephen but there was no blood drawn. He patiently suffered in silence until he was able to release her back into her cage, before letting out a succession of 'Ow! Ow! Ow!' exclamations as he clutched his bruised thumb.

Once I had collected my sample, I dissolved the beak fragments in some mineral oil on a glass slide. A few minutes later, I was able to look at a highly magnified view of the debris under my microscope. The cause of the problem could be seen at once. I could see a tiny spider-like mite, known as cnemidocoptes, or more commonly, the scaly face mite. The mite feeds on the debris around the base of the beak, and also sometimes on other parts of the budgie's body such as the legs and feet. It is a common mite in young birds, and it rapidly spreads from bird to bird. If left untreated, the signs gradually worsen, with the beak becoming increasingly distorted and misshapen, and the skin on the legs growing coarser and thickened. Home remedies don't work: the only answer is a potent modern anti-parasite drug.

The only readily available version of this drug at the time was an injection marketed for parasite control in cattle. I had to use this highly diluted in sterile water, according to a formula worked out from the experiences of specialised bird vets and published in veterinary textbooks. Once I'd made up this solution, I placed a single drop on the skin on the back of the Flap's neck. She didn't notice as I did it: it's like an injection without a needle. The drug is absorbed through the skin into the bloodstream, and it spreads throughout the body. It is highly effective, killing all mites in the budgie, both in the beak, and also any that may be lurking in the legs or feet. I had to give Flutter the same treatment, and poor Stephen received another 'budgie bite' as he held her steady for this.

Scaly face mites are often deeply engrained in a bird's tissues, and a series of treatments is needed to eradicate them completely. Sometimes owners apply the medicine themselves after the first dose, but Stephen wanted to be absolutely certain that it was done thoroughly, so he brought the two birds back to see me each week, for four weeks in a row. The positive effect of the drugs kicked in almost at once: both birds stopped scraping their beaks as often as they had been. And every week, I could see an improvement in the quality of their beaks. By the time of the last application, their beaks had a clear, shiny surface again.

After the first incident, Stephen was better prepared: for each subsequent veterinary visit, he came properly equipped. Complex animal restraint methods such as muzzles, collars and chains aren't needed for budgies: a simple pair of gardening gloves was all that Stephen needed to protect the tender flesh at the base of his thumb.

Questions and answers on cage birds

Budgies are the most popular avian pet: 'cheap and cheerful' (or perhaps 'cheep and cheerful') is a good way of describing them. I've been asked many questions about cage birds via The Telegraph *column: here's a selection.*

My thirteen-year-old daughter has just been given a young budgie by a friend. The problem is that the bird does not seem to have enough feathers on his tail and wings, and he can only just manage to flutter up onto the lowest perch in the cage. I would have expected that he should be able to fly easily from perch to perch. When I phoned the friend, I was told that the bird had 'French Moult'. What is this and what should we do?

AW by email

'French Moult' is a common disease of young budgies, frequently caused by the polyoma virus. The virus is a very serious problem to have in an aviary, but it is not fatal to individual birds unless they are very young. Instead, it causes varying degrees of feather abnormalities, which often resolve with the passage of time. Infected birds can become very tame because their lack of ability to fly can make them more dependent on humans. If your daughter wants a fully healthy bird, she should give this one back, and buy another from a different source. However, she may prefer to nurture this sick bird, in the hope that within a year he will become a very tame, normal-looking bird who can fly properly. He may be infectious to other birds, so he must be kept in isolation, which is fine as long as he gets plenty of human company.

> My mother's three-year-old budgie has started regurgitating his food and splashing the resultant mess all over his head. My vet suggested that it is due to his urge to breed, and on his advice we removed his mirror from the cage and lowered the temperature of the room. He is now better but he has stopped talking, only saying hello in the morning when he is woken up. He used to talk a lot, as well as reciting nursery rhymes. The vet has suggested that we get another bird, but we are afraid that if we do this he will stop talking for ever. Is there such a thing as bromide for budgies or what can we do?
>
> JP, Poulton-le-Fylde

It certainly sounds as if the budgie is under the influence of his hormones at the moment, and you can't easily neuter him, nor is there medication that will help. In his mind, the budgie is 'feeding another bird' when he regurgitates.

Budgies often do this to objects that they are fond of, and your mother is lucky that he is not regurgitating onto her, as often happens. Budgies are very social creatures, living in large flocks in the wild. For his sake, it would be best to get another budgie as a friend for him. He may or may not talk as much as before – this behaviour is unpredictable – but he will definitely be a happier bird. My impression of talking birds is that they do it more when they are happy, but please do let me know how you get on. Make sure your mother still spends time talking to him, to increase the chances of him remembering the words.

> Our six-year-old budgie has developed a lump at the base of his abdomen, which I suspect may be a tumour and which will ultimately prove fatal. I am wondering if anyone actually consults a vet for such little birds, given that under the fluff there is hardly anything there to operate on. She is so full of life I wonder if there is anything that can be done in a case such as this.
>
> DL, Nottinghamshire

You're probably correct in both your diagnosis and your prognosis: the average lifespan of budgies is five to eight years, so your bird may be nearing the end of his allotted span. It is certainly possible to do plenty to treat budgies and other tiny animals: their diminutive size can make anaesthesia and surgery fiddly and complicated, but it can be done. Money is often the deciding factor: people may justify spending £500 on the family dog, but they find it more difficult to pay out such sums on small family pets that often have short lives in any case. If you do decide to consult a vet, it's worth seeking out someone with a strong avian interest.

Acknowledgements

I'm passionate about my profession: I was born with a sense that I had to be a vet, informing my parents of this ambition when I was just five years old. I've always felt a connection with animals: they are us, in a different type of body, with different ways of communicating. They can't look after themselves, and we have responsibilities as humans to care for them. As a vet, I've been part of the system for caring for them, and it's as rewarding a vocation as I can imagine.

I've been blessed to be part of a team that really cares: my veterinary partners Andrew and Nicola have made it their life's objective to provide the best possible care for our patients. And the other vets who work with us – Ciara, Emiliana, Jean, Ellen and others – have shared this ambition. Our supporting team of veterinary nurses, receptionists and office staff are like the skeleton that supports the body: we couldn't do it without them.

I've also been blessed with a family that cares about animals: my wife Joyce trained as a midwife and has an instinctive commitment to ensure the welfare of those unable to care for themselves. We couldn't have managed the menagerie that makes up our home without her support and hard work: as well as dogs and cats, we've had hens, ducks, an aviary full of canaries, finches and budgies, rabbits, guinea pigs, rats, snakes, gerbils and goldfish. My daughters, Anna and Ella, have been brought up around animals, and their natural enthusiasm for the company of other species has been a joy to witness.

The life of a vet is a calling; it isn't for everyone, but it has definitely been for me. I can't imagine a more rewarding, fulfilling job than caring for other species. They can't talk, they can't explain themselves, they can't complain and they can't express gratitude. But they do need help, just as any human with medical problems needs help. And to be one of those lucky ones who can offer that help to them has been – and still is – an honour.

So my final word of thanks goes to the animals who feature in this book, and indeed to their owners. My life wouldn't have any stories if it were not for the many animals who have shared their lives and experiences with my own.